TALKING TO THE SUN

AN ILLUSTRATED ANTHOLOGY OF
POEMS FOR YOUNG PEOPLE

————SELECTED AND INTRODUCED BY————

KENNETH KOCH AND KATE FARRELL

THE METROPOLITAN MUSEUM OF ART
HENRY HOLT AND COMPANY
NEW YORK

We thank Barbara Anderman, consulting editor in the Department of Special Publications at The Metropolitan Museum of Art, whose idea this book originally was and who did so much of the work that made it possible. She helped us select the works of art, she edited the text, and she watched over the whole project with intelligence, sensitivity, and patience. We also thank Miriam Berman, who designed the book, and, for their essential help in various ways, Robie Rogge, Cynthia Schaffner, Elizabeth Van Doren, and all of the staff of the Department of Special Publications. Thanks, too, to Robert Blumberg for his generous help and advice.

KF
KK

Front cover: The Repast of the Lion *(detail). Henri Rousseau, French, 1844–1910. Oil on canvas*
Back cover: Detail of a dust jacket for La vie de Montmartre *by Montorgueil, 1899. Pierre Vidal, French, 1849–1929*

All the works of art in this book, with three exceptions, were photographed by The Metropolitan Museum of Art Photograph Studio. The photograph on page 61, number 77, was taken by Malcolm Varon, N.Y.C.; the photograph on page 68, number 96, was taken by Lee Boltin; and the photograph on page 68, number 97, was taken by Bob Hanson.

For acknowledgments of the use of copyrighted material, see page 107.

Published by The Metropolitan Museum of Art, New York, and
Henry Holt and Company, Inc., 521 Fifth Avenue, New York, New York 10175
Published simultaneously in Canada

Produced by the Department of Special Publications,
The Metropolitan Museum of Art
Typeset by Advance Graphic, New York
Printed and bound by A. Mondadori, Verona, Italy
Designed by Miriam Berman

Library of Congress Cataloging-in-Publication Data
Main entry under title:

Talking to the sun.

Includes indexes.
Summary: Poems from various time periods and many countries are organized by theme and illustrated with reproductions of art works from the Metropolitan Museum of Art in New York.
1. Children's poetry. 2. Art—Juvenile literature.
3. Metropolitan Museum of Art (New York, N.Y.)
[1. Poetry—Collections. 2. Art] I. Koch, Kenneth, 1925–   II. Farrell, Kate. III. Metropolitan Museum of Art (New York, N.Y.)
PN6109.97.T35 1985   808.81'0088054   85–15428
ISBN 0-87099-436-0
ISBN 0-8050-0144-1 (Henry Holt)

10 9 8 7 6 5 4 3

PREFACE

To find the poems in this book, we looked at poetry written in English from the fifteenth century on; at poems written in other languages—French, Italian, Spanish, German, Russian, Chinese, Japanese; at tribal poems and chants from African and American-Indian cultures; at ancient poems from Egypt and India. There are a good many modern poems, enough to give an idea of what modern poetry is like; there are poems by many of the greatest poets who have written in any language: Shakespeare, Blake, Keats, Shelley, Hopkins, Dante, Rimbaud, Leopardi, Rilke, Lorca, Tu Fu, and Li Po (among others). There are many different kinds of poetry: magic incantations, lullabies, love songs, nonsense poems, and poems about nature, about animals, about cities. There are poems in many different forms: haiku, sonnets, long poems and short ones, poems that rhyme, and poems that do not. Our aim was a book that would show how great and how likable poetry is and what a variety of it there is to read.

Kenneth Koch

CONTENTS

INTRODUCTION, 6

HYMN TO THE SUN

Hymn to the Sun, *Fang people,* 8
Poems to the Sun, *Ancient Egypt,* 9
Song for the Sun That Disappeared behind the
    Rainclouds, *Hottentot people,* 9
Five Ghost Songs, *Ambo people,* 10
O Beauteous One, *Ancient Egypt,* 10
There Are No People Song, *Navaho Indians,* 11
Song of the Flood, *Navaho Indians,* 12
The Approach of the Storm,
    Chippewa Indians, 12
House Song to the East, *Navaho Indians,* 13

COME UNTO THESE YELLOW SANDS

Come unto These Yellow Sands,
    William Shakespeare, 14
Spring, the Sweet Spring, *Thomas Nashe,* 15
Under the Greenwood Tree,
    William Shakespeare, 15
How Marigolds Came Yellow, *Robert Herrick,* 16
How Violets Came Blue, *Robert Herrick,* 16
The Argument of His Book, *Robert Herrick,* 16
To Daffodils, *Robert Herrick,* 17
The Locust Tree in Flower,
    William Carlos Williams, 18
Spring, *William Blake,* 18
Another Sarah, *Anne Porter,* 19
We Like March, *Emily Dickinson,* 19
I Think, *James Schuyler,* 20
Spring, *Reed Bye,* 21

ALL THE PRETTY LITTLE HORSES

All the Pretty Little Horses, *Anonymous,* 22
Lullaby, *Akan people,* 23
Song of Parents Who Want to Wake up
    Their Son, *Kwakiutl Indians,* 23

Puva, puva, puva, *Hopi Indians,* 23
Lully, Lulla, *Anonymous,* 24
The Song of Kuk-ook, the Bad Boy, *Eskimo,* 24
To Mistress Isabel Pennell, *John Skelton,* 25
The Cottager to Her Infant,
    Dorothy Wordsworth, 26
Minnie and Winnie, *Alfred, Lord Tennyson,* 26
From a Childhood, *Rainer Maria Rilke,* 27
Silly Song, *Federico García Lorca,* 28
Miss Blues'es Child, *Langston Hughes,* 28
Kirsten, *Ted Berrigan,* 29
Poem for Shane on Her Brother's Birthday,
    Donald T. Sanders, 30
Autobiographia Literaria, *Frank O'Hara,* 31

COME LIVE WITH ME AND BE MY LOVE

The Passionate Shepherd to His Love,
    Christopher Marlowe, 33
Although I Conquer All the Earth,
    Ancient India, 33
The River-Merchant's Wife: A Letter,
    Ezra Pound (after Li Po), 34
Oath of Friendship, *Anonymous,* 35
Sonnet, *Dante Alighieri,* 36
Phillida and Coridon, *Nicholas Breton,* 37
It Was a Lover and His Lass,
    William Shakespeare, 38
Upon Julia's Clothes, *Robert Herrick,* 38
A Ternary of Littles, upon a Pipkin of
    Jelly Sent to a Lady, *Robert Herrick,* 39
I Have Lived and I Have Loved, *Anonymous,* 39
Greensleeves, *Anonymous,* 40
Indian Serenade, *Percy Bysshe Shelley,* 41
A Birthday, *Christina Rossetti,* 41
To an Isle in the Water, *William Butler Yeats,* 42
The Letter, *Alfred, Lord Tennyson,* 43
Oh, When I Was in Love with You,
    A. E. Housman, 44
Hops, *Boris Pasternak,* 44
I Want to Say Your Name,
    Léopold Sédar Senghor, 45

Sunday, *James Schuyler,* 46
Juke Box Love Song, *Langston Hughes,* 46
Song, *Frank O'Hara,* 47

WHEN THE GREEN WOODS LAUGH

When the Green Woods Laugh, *William Blake,* 48
The Koocoo, *Anonymous,* 49
If All the World Were Paper, *Anonymous,* 49
A Nut Tree, *Anonymous,* 50
Meet-on-the-Road, *Anonymous,* 50
Bingo, *Anonymous,* 51
I'll Sail upon the Dog-star, *Thomas Durfey,* 51
Humpty Dumpty's Recitation, *Lewis Carroll,* 52
The Big Rock Candy Mountains,
    American folksong, 53
Jabberwocky, *Lewis Carroll,* 53
The Owl and the Pussy-cat, *Edward Lear,* 54
"I Am Cherry Alive," the Little Girl Sang,
    Delmore Schwartz, 54
Counting-Out Rhyme, *Edna St. Vincent Millay,* 55
Today, *Frank O'Hara,* 55

A RABBIT AS KING OF THE GHOSTS

A Rabbit as King of the Ghosts, *Wallace Stevens,* 56
The Magnificent Bull, *Dinka people,* 57
Ground-Squirrel Song, *Navaho Indians,* 57
I Sing for the Animals, *Teton Sioux Indians,* 57
The War God's Horse Song, *Navaho Indians,* 58
I Stood in the Maytime Meadows, *Anonymous,* 59
From The Unicorn, *Rainer Maria Rilke,* 59
To Ride, *Paul Eluard,* 59
The White Horse, *D. H. Lawrence,* 59
Engraved on the Collar of a Dog, Which I Gave
    to His Royal Highness, *Alexander Pope,* 60
here's a little mouse, *e. e. cummings,* 60
Autumn Cove, *Li Po,* 61
The Tyger, *William Blake,* 61
The Fallow Deer at the Lonely House,
    Thomas Hardy, 61

4

Poem, *William Carlos Williams,* 62
From Jubilate Agno, *Christopher Smart,* 62
The Owl, *Hopi Indians,* 63
Wild Goose, Wild Goose, *Issa,* 63
The Cat and the Moon, *William Butler Yeats,* 63
Meditations of a Parrot, *John Ashbery,* 64
Peacock, *D. H. Lawrence,* 64
Butterfly, *D. H. Lawrence,* 65
They look/like newlyweds, *Ryōta,* 65
Where the Bee Sucks, *William Shakespeare,* 66
Grasshoppers, *John Clare,* 66
Bee! I'm Expecting You!, *Emily Dickinson,* 66
Spider, *Bashō,* 66
On the Grasshopper and Cricket, *John Keats,* 67
Three Animals, *Ron Padgett,* 67
Pig, *Paul Eluard,* 68
Little Fish, *D. H. Lawrence,* 68
How Doth the Little Crocodile, *Lewis Carroll,* 68
From Elephant, *Pablo Neruda,* 69
The Elephant, *Yoruba people,* 69

THE WORLD'S WANDERERS

The World's Wanderers, *Percy Bysshe Shelley,* 70
Still Night Thoughts, *Li Po,* 71
Spring Night in Lo-yang—Hearing a Flute, *Li Po,* 71
They Say You're Staying in a Mountain Temple,
    Tu Fu, 71
Thinking of East Mountain, *Li Po,* 71
Viewing the Waterfall at Mount Lu, *Li Po,* 71
So, We'll Go No More A-Roving, *Lord Byron,* 72
To the Moon, *Giacomo Leopardi,* 72
To the Moon, *Percy Bysshe Shelley,* 72
Waiting Both, *Thomas Hardy,* 73
The Moon Rises, *Federico García Lorca,* 73
Silver, *Walter de la Mare,* 73
Heaven, *George Herbert,* 74
I Wandered Lonely as a Cloud, *William
    Wordsworth,* 75
From To a Skylark, *William Wordsworth,* 75
The Wind Took up the Northern Things,
    Emily Dickinson, 75

Sensation, *Arthur Rimbaud,* 76
Stopping by Woods on a Snowy Evening,
    Robert Frost, 76
The Waking, *Theodore Roethke,* 77
Afternoon on a Hill, *Edna St. Vincent Millay,* 77

FOR THE MOMENT

For the Moment, *Pierre Reverdy,* 78
I've just come up, *Jōsō,* 79
Well, let's go, *Bashō,* 79
First cold rain, *Bashō,* 79
May rains, *Sanpū,* 79
On the temple bell, *Buson,* 79
No one spoke, *Ryōta,* 79
Beside the road, *Bashō,* 79
How cool it feels, *Bashō,* 79
One person, *Issa,* 79
From Song of Myself, *Walt Whitman,* 80
To a Poor Old Woman,
    William Carlos Williams, 81
Cuckoo, *Gerard Manley Hopkins,* 81
The Red Wheelbarrow,
    William Carlos Williams, 81
Song, *James Schuyler,* 81
In a Train, *Robert Bly,* 82
The Pasture, *Robert Frost,* 82
Some Good Things to Be Said for the Iron Age,
    Gary Snyder, 82
Chocolate Milk, *Ron Padgett,* 83
Ballad of the Morning Streets, *Amiri Baraka,* 83
Song Form, *Amiri Baraka,* 83
Convalescence, *Noël Coward,* 84
The Wind Is Blowing West, *Joseph Ceravolo,* 84

SLEEPING ON THE CEILING

Sleeping on the Ceiling, *Elizabeth Bishop,* 86
Dawn, *Arthur Rimbaud,* 87
Who Is the East?, *Emily Dickinson,* 87
The Most Beautiful, *Guido Gozzano,* 88

The Song of Wandering Aengus,
    William Butler Yeats, 89
Rose, Oh Pure Contradiction,
    Rainer Maria Rilke, 89
Disillusionment of Ten O'clock,
    Wallace Stevens, 90
The Great Figure, *William Carlos Williams,* 90
From Free Union, *André Breton,* 91
Bavarian Gentians, *D. H. Lawrence,* 91
From Liberty, *Paul Eluard,* 92
Mr. Lizard Is Crying, *Federico García Lorca,* 93
Narcolepsy, *Maureen Owen,* 94
Fog, *Carl Sandburg,* 94
Canticle, *David Shapiro,* 95

TENDER BUTTONS

From Tender Buttons, *Gertrude Stein,* 97
Heart Crown and Mirror,
    Guillaume Apollinaire, 98
Vowels, *Arthur Rimbaud,* 98
It's Raining, *Guillaume Apollinaire,* 99
Ploughing on Sunday, *Wallace Stevens,* 100
Pied Beauty, *Gerard Manley Hopkins,* 101
up into the silence the green, *e. e. cummings,* 101
Sporting Goods, *Philippe Soupault,* 102
The Thinnest Shadow, *John Ashbery,* 102
Poem, *Frank O'Hara,* 103
A True Account of Talking to the Sun at Fire
    Island, *Frank O'Hara,* 104

APPENDIX, 106
ACKNOWLEDGMENTS, 107
CREDITS, 108
INDEX OF AUTHORS AND TITLES, 110
INDEX OF FIRST LINES, 111

INTRODUCTION

ABOUT ART AND POETRY

Everyone has feelings, thoughts, wishes, instincts, and sensations that seem almost impossible to talk about or to express in a way that seems absolutely complete and true. Even supposedly ordinary, everyday things can be secretly very important but hard to talk about. Think, for instance, of trying to describe exactly the thrill of riding a bicycle down a breezy hill, the peacefulness of holding your cat on your lap after a long day at school, the strangeness of your first memories of your house or street, the happiness of discovering something—a stream in the woods or the first tree buds of spring. Think of trying to explain the confused excitement of feeling secretly in love with someone across the room; the mystery of language, of color, of beauty, of time going by; the funny wildness of dreams, fantasies, daydreams; and the loneliness, sometimes, of wondering about yourself and the whole universe in a way that you can't explain. Many, many of the things that people care about the most are very hard to talk about. Everyone's experience of the world is mostly private and not quite like anyone else's, so it is hard to communicate that experience in an ordinary, logical way. The urge to express the absolute truth about the way things are in one's own, private, inner world of thoughts, feelings, and imagination is one of the reasons why poets write poetry, painters paint pictures, and composers write music. The arts are natural and exciting expressions of these things. People count on the arts to tell them the truth about what it is to be a person in the world—a world that we are always wondering about and never completely understand. In a way, the pleasure of good painting or sculpture or poetry is a little like the pleasure of seeing through the eyes of someone who can see in a way that no one else has ever seen before, the excitement of imagining with someone else's strange and brilliant imagination, or the surprise of remembering with someone else's memory.

ABOUT READING POETRY

It is as natural to like reading poetry as it is to like looking at paintings or listening to music, but it is helpful to know what to expect from poetry since you *read* it and that makes it a little different from art forms that you look at or listen to. A painter uses paint, a sculptor uses stone, a composer uses sound, and a poet uses words. He uses words in a different way from the way people use them in ordinary conversation and writing, just as a painter who is an artist uses paint in a different way from a housepainter, and a sculptor uses stone in a different way from a stonemason. All artists, including poets, want to make a different kind of sense. Poetry, like the other arts and like your strangest dreams, comes from the imagination, where there is a different kind of logic and a different kind of sense.

Reading poetry, like writing poetry, is a creative activity, one in which you use your own imagination. That is one of the reasons why reading poetry is so satisfying. When you like a poem (or a statue, a piece of music, a scene in a play), the pleasure you feel probably comes from the way the work affects your imagination. It's a little like the pleasure of daydreaming. In fact, it's fine to daydream a little as you read or listen to a poem, the way you might daydream a little as you watch a dance, or wander through the rooms of a beautiful building, or listen to a song or to a friend's conversation.

Every good poet writes a kind of poetry that is new and different from the poetry of any other poet, because it comes from an imagination that isn't like anybody else's. When you first read a good poet's work, it's a little like meeting a strange and interesting friend. Discovering what a new friend—or a new kind of poetry—is like is a pleasure.

If a poem seems hard, the first thing to do is to read it over several times to get used to the way the words go together. Often that is enough to make it clear. Sometimes there are words in a poem that you don't recognize; you can look these up in a dictionary or ask someone about them. Sometimes, too, a poem seems strange because it was written in another time, when people spoke in a different way or wrote poetry in a different way from the way people do now. Again, you can ask someone about these things.

Because poetry is made with words and words already have meaning in a way that paint strokes, for instance, or dance steps or musical notes don't, people sometimes worry about what a poem "really means." Different poems mean different things to different people at different times, but that isn't something that you need to think about when you read a poem. In fact, worrying about finding the "right" meaning can get in the way of your liking and understanding poetry. Just as you don't have to understand everything about your friends in order to enjoy them and to learn things from them, so you don't have to understand everything about a poem to like it and get something from it. Whatever you get from a poem is fine. Maybe you'll like a kind of strangeness, for instance, or a poem's sound, its words, its subject, the way it goes from one line to the next, or the mood it puts you in. Maybe you'll like the way it seems to get something just right; or what it makes

you remember, and think about, and feel; or the way it makes you suddenly understand something more clearly. Poetry can be satisfying and exciting while it remains a little mysterious.

One of the joys of poetry is that all the new experience and knowledge that you bring to it as you get older and learn more and change make it mean more to you. That is one of the reasons why people come back to good poetry and read it again and again.

You don't have to be a poet to write poetry any more than you have to be a painter to paint a picture, and nothing helps you to like and understand poetry as much as writing it yourself. So if this book inspires you to begin writing poetry or painting, so much the better.

ABOUT THIS BOOK

Poetry has been inspired by many different kinds of things and has been written in many different ways. It changes—as the other arts change—not only because different poets write different kinds of poetry, but because poets have lived in different times and places. A landscape looks one way from horseback, another way when it's disappearing through the clouds below you after a jet takeoff. April isn't the same through the chilly window of a medieval castle as it is when you look out from a heated room in a city skyscraper. As the world changes, the way people write about it, draw it, and paint it changes. This is something you can see in the poems and works of art in this book. The organization of *Talking to the Sun* into ten sections was suggested by the history of poetry; the book starts with ancient and primitive poetry and ends with modern poetry. But since poetry, however much it changes with time, has

always been inspired by similar things— love, for instance, and the seasons—there are poems from various times in almost all of the sections.

The illustrations in this book are all reproductions of works of art in the collections of The Metropolitan Museum of Art. We selected the poems first and then chose works of art to go with them. The art was chosen not to illustrate the poetry literally, but to add to the reader's enjoyment of it, with the idea that the poetry would do the same thing for the visual works in the book. The sentences that I wrote to introduce each section and accompany some of the poems are there for that reason too—not to limit understanding, but to explain something that might not otherwise be clear about the poems, or to show another way to think of them. We have also included the dates of the poets and artists; sometimes just knowing that a poem or a painting was created in the seventeenth century rather than the twentieth century explains why it is the way it is.

Naturally, you don't have to read a book like this in any order. You may like some poems better than others and want to read them over and over; a certain kind of art may appeal to you now, another kind later. What you like will probably change as you change, and this is a book that we hope you will enjoy for a long time.

Keep in mind that the pictures are reproductions of works of art and it is always better to see the original art if you can. You might want to visit an art museum like The Metropolitan Museum of Art; you might want, too, to find other books of poetry in bookshops and libraries.

Kate Farrell

Many of the first poems known to us are magical chants that praise nature or explain things that people didn't understand about nature—why the sun rises and sets, for example, or why there is thunder. Often these chants were intended to bring good fortune—to make crops grow or to bring sunshine or rain.

HYMN TO THE SUN

The fearful night sinks
Trembling into the depth
Before your lightning eye
And the rapid arrows
From your fiery quiver.
With sparking blows of light
You tear her cloak
The black cloak lined with fire
And studded with gleaming
    stars—
With sparking blows of light
You tear the black cloak.

Fang people, Africa

The sun in this poem is a fabulous warrior who defeats his enemy, the night, with blazing arrows of sunlight.

1

POEMS TO THE SUN

All the cattle are resting in the fields,
The trees and the plants are growing,
The birds flutter above the marshes,
Their wings uplifted in adoration,
And all the sheep are dancing,
All winged things are flying,
They live when you have shone on them.

•

The boats sail upstream and downstream alike,
Every highway is open because you dawn.
The fish in the river leap up in front of you,
Your rays are in the middle of the great green sea.

Ancient Egypt

SONG FOR THE SUN THAT DISAPPEARED BEHIND THE RAINCLOUDS

The fire darkens, the wood turns black.
The flame extinguishes, misfortune upon us.
God sets out in search of the sun.
The rainbow sparkles in his hand,
The bow of the divine hunter.
He has heard the lamentations of his children.
He walks along the milky way, he collects the stars.
With quick arms he piles them into a basket
Piles them up with quick arms
Like a woman who collects lizards
And piles them into her pot, piles them
Until the pot overflows with lizards
Until the basket overflows with light.

Hottentot people, Africa

1 *Autumn Landscape*.
Stained-glass window.
New York, Tiffany
Studios, 1923

2 *Red Sunset on the
Dnieper* (detail).
Arkhip Ivanovich
Kuindji, Russian,
1842–1910. Oil on
canvas

FIVE GHOST SONGS

The dove stays in the garden.
Oh, you dove,
Oh, that dove.

• • •

I have no rattles—
Am shabby for the shades.

• • •

The ghost is gone in rags,
The ghost is gone in rags,
And the ghost in rags,
The ghost is gone in rags.

• • •

See how it circles—
The airplane on its airdrome.

• • •

Ah! the roofs,
Ah! Ah! Ah! Ah! Ah! Ah!
She climbs the roofs,
Our mother.
My friends?
Why do you call me?
The boy sleeps in the bush,
Oh . . . Oh . . . Oh
This is like a swing.

Ambo people, Africa

*The people carved under this drum
look fearful and uneasy, as if they
(like the people who might have
sung these songs) might be sensing
the presence of something invisible
and unknown and unpredictable.*

3

4

O BEAUTEOUS ONE

O beauteous one, O cow, O great one,
O great magician, O splendid lady, O queen of gods!
The King reveres you, Pharaoh, give that he live!
O queen of gods, he reveres you, give that he live!

Behold him, Hathor, mistress, from heaven,
See him, Hathor, mistress, from lightland,
Hear him, flaming one, from ocean!
Behold him, queen of gods, from sky, from earth,
From Nubia, from Libya, from Manu, from Bakhu,
From each land, from each place, where your majesty shines!

Behold what is in his inmost,
Though his mouth speaks not;
His heart is straight, his inmost open,
No darkness is in his breast!
He reveres you, O queen of gods,
Give that he live!

Ancient Egypt

*This chant pleads for prosperity on earth from the queen of the gods, the
divine cow, whose image is pictured here.*

10

THERE ARE NO PEOPLE SONG

You say there were no people.
　　Smoke was spreading over the earth.
You say there were no people.
　　Smoke was spreading.

First Man was the very first to emerge, they say,
　　Smoke was spreading.
He brought with him the various robes and precious things,
　they say,
　　Smoke was spreading.
He brought with him the white corn and the yellow corn,
　they say,
　　Smoke was spreading.
He brought with him the various animals and the growing
　things, they say,
　　Smoke was spreading.

You say there were no people.
　　Smoke was spreading.

First Woman was the very first to emerge, they say,
　　Smoke was spreading.
She brought with her the various precious things and robes,
　they say,
　　Smoke was spreading.
She brought with her the yellow corn and the varicolored
　corn, they say,
　　Smoke was spreading.
She brought with her the various animals and the growing
　things, they say,
　　Smoke was spreading.

You say there were no people.
　　Smoke was spreading.
You say there were no people.
　　Smoke was spreading.

Navaho Indians, North America

The image here is of a sphinx, a strange, primitive, imaginary creature. The poem is a primitive, imaginary story about the arrival on earth of the first man and the first women.

3 Drum. Wood, carved and painted. Congo, Vili people, 19th century

4 Head from a statue of a cow goddess. Porphyritic diorite. Egyptian, Dynasty 18, ca. 1417–1379 B.C.

5 Sphinx of Amenhotpe III. Blue faience. Egyptian, Dynasty 18, ca. 1417–1379 B.C.

5

6

SONG OF THE FLOOD

The first man—you are his child, he is your child.
The first woman—you are his child, he is your child.
The water monster—you are his child, he is your child.
The black sea-horse—you are his child, he is your child.
The black snake—you are his child, he is your child.
The big blue snake—you are his child, he is your child.
The white corn—you are his child, he is your child.
The yellow corn—you are his child, he is your child.
The corn pollen—you are his child, he is your child.
The corn beetle—you are his child, he is your child.
Sabanahray—you are his child, he is your child.
Bekayhozhon—you are his child, he is your child.

Navaho Indians, North America

Since nature is endlessly being reborn—the corn turns to seed and becomes the next year's corn, the mother has a child who grows up and becomes a mother—there is a unity and continuity in nature that people have always wondered about.

7

THE APPROACH OF THE STORM

From the half
Of the sky
That which lives there
Is coming, and makes a noise.

Chippewa Indians, North America

The storm in this poem is an imaginary animal who comes out of an imaginary cave in the sky, growling, perhaps, like thunder.

HOUSE SONG TO THE EAST

Far in the east, far below,
  there a house was made;
    Delightful house.
God of Dawn,
  there his house was made;
    Delightful house.
The Dawn,
  there his house was made;
    Delightful house.
White Corn,
  there its house was made;
    Delightful house.
Soft possessions,
  for them a house was made;
    Delightful house.
Water in plenty, surrounding,
  for it a house was made;
    Delightful house.
Corn pollen,
  for it a house was made;
    Delightful house.
The ancients make
  their presence delightful;
    Delightful house.

Before me, may it be delightful.
Behind me, may it be delightful.
Around me, may it be delightful.
Below me, may it be delightful.
Above me, may it be delightful.
All, may it be delightful.

        Navaho Indians, North America

This early poem is a happy vision of the beauty, peace, and safety of an ideal house, which is also suggested, perhaps, by this twentieth-century painting.

6 Mother and child. Wood.
  Mali, Bamana people,
  19th–20th century

7 Gender (xylophone) in the form
  of a two-headed dragon. Wood,
  metal, and bamboo. Javanese,
  19th century

8 *Garden at Vaucresson*. Edouard
  Vuillard, French, 1868–1940.
  Tempera on canvas

8

Poets and artists have always been inspired by the beauty of spring, by the possibility of happiness that spring suggests with all its new growth and light and color.

COME UNTO THESE YELLOW SANDS

Come unto these yellow sands,
And then take hands:
Curtsied when you have, and kissed,
The wild waves whist:
Foot it featly here and there,
And, sweet sprites, the burden bear.
Hark, hark, bow wow:
The watch-dogs bark, bow wow.
Hark, hark, I hear,
The strain of strutting Chanticleer
Cry Cock-a-diddle-dow.

William Shakespeare, 1564–1616

UNDER THE GREENWOOD TREE

Under the greenwood tree,
    Who loves to lie with me,
    And turn his merry note
    Unto the sweet bird's throat
Come hither, come hither, come hither:
    Here shall he see
    No enemy
But winter and rough weather.

Who doth ambition shun,
    And loves to live i' the sun.
    Seeking the food he eats,
    And pleased with what he gets,
Come hither, come hither, come hither:
    Here shall he see
    No enemy
But winter and rough weather.

William Shakespeare

SPRING, THE SWEET SPRING

Spring, the sweet spring, is the year's pleasant king;
Then blooms each thing, then maids dance in a ring,
Cold doth not sting, the pretty birds do sing:
    Cuckoo, jug-jug, pu-we, to-witta-woo!

The palm and may make country houses gay,
Lambs frisk and play, the shepherds pipe all day,
And we hear aye birds tune this merry lay:
    Cuckoo, jug-jug, pu-we, to-witta-woo!

The fields breathe sweet, the daisies kiss our feet,
Young lovers meet, old wives a-sunning sit,
In every street these tunes our ears do greet:
    Cuckoo, jug-jug, pu-we, to-witta-woo!
      Spring, the sweet spring!

Thomas Nashe, 1567–1601

9 *Nasturtiums and "The Dance."* Henri Matisse, French,
  1869–1954. Oil on canvas, 1912

10 Hand-tinted lithograph from *L'An* by Thomas Braun.
   Franz M. Melchers, Belgian, 1868–1944. Brussels,
   E. Lyon-Claesen, 1897

11 *Peach Blossoms—Villiers le Bel* (detail). Childe Hassam,
   American, 1859–1935. Oil on canvas

These poems give an imaginary explanation of how marigolds became yellow and violets blue.

HOW MARIGOLDS CAME YELLOW

Jealous girls these sometimes were,
While they liv'd, or lasted here:
Turn'd to flowers, still they be
Yellow, marked for jealousy.

Robert Herrick

HOW VIOLETS CAME BLUE

Love on a day (wise poets tell)
    Some time in wrangling spent,
Whether the violets should excel,
    Or she, in sweetest scent.

But Venus having lost the day,
    Poor girls, she fell on you
And beat you so, (as some dare say)
    Her blows did make you blue.

Robert Herrick

13

12

THE ARGUMENT OF HIS BOOK

I sing of brooks, of blossoms, birds, and bowers:
Of April, May, of June, and July flowers.
I sing of Maypoles, hock-carts, wassails, wakes,
Of bridegrooms, brides, and of their bridal cakes.
I write of youth, of love, and have access
By these, to sing of cleanly wantonness.
I sing of dews, of rains, and piece by piece
Of balm, of oil, of spice, and ambergris.
I sing of times trans-shifting; and I write
How roses first came red, and lilies white.
I write of groves, of twilights, and I sing
The court of Mab, and of the fairy king.
I write of Hell; I sing (and ever shall)
Of Heaven, and hope to have it after all.

Robert Herrick, 1591–1674

This, the first poem in a book by Robert Herrick, mentions many of the subjects the poet writes about.

TO DAFFODILS

Fair daffodils we weep to see
    You haste away so soon:
As yet the early-rising sun
    Has not attain'd his noon.
      Stay, stay,
    Until the hasting day
      Has run
    But to the evensong;
And, having pray'd together, we
    Will go with you along.

We have short time to stay, as you,
    We have as short a spring;
As quick a growth to meet decay,
    As you, or any thing.
      We die,
    As your hours do, and dry
      Away,
    Like to the summer's rain;
Or as the pearls of morning's dew
    Ne'er to be found again.

Robert Herrick

12 Detail of "The Start of the Hunt,"
one of a series of seven tapestries
entitled *The Hunt of the Unicorn.*
Silk, wool, and metal thread.
French or Flemish, ca. 1500

13 Detail of "The Unicorn Defends
Himself," one of a series of seven
tapestries entitled *The Hunt of the
Unicorn.* Silk, wool, and metal
thread. French or Flemish, ca. 1500

14 *The Flowering Orchard* (detail).
Vincent van Gogh, Dutch,
1853–1890. Oil on canvas, 1888

14

15

THE LOCUST TREE IN FLOWER

Among
of
green

stiff
old
bright

broken
branch
come

white
sweet
May

again

William Carlos Williams
1883–1963

The bare look of this poem, with one small word on each line, suggests the look of a locust tree in the early spring, with the first tiny blossoms appearing on bare branches.

15 *Flowering Plum and Orchid.* After Yün Shou-p'ing (1633–1690), Chinese. Detail of a handscroll, *The Hundred Flowers.* Ink and colors on silk, 18th century

16 Details of a color lithograph. Vienna, the Wiener Werkstätte, early 20th century

17 *The Parc Monceau, Paris.* Claude Monet, French, 1840–1926. Oil on canvas, 1876

SPRING

Sound the Flute!
Now it's mute.
Birds delight
Day and Night;
Nightingale
In the dale,
Lake in Sky,
Merrily,
Merrily, Merrily to welcome in the Year.

Little Boy
Full of joy;
Little Girl,
Sweet and small;
Cock does crow,
So do you;
Merry voice,
Infant noise,
Merrily, Merrily to welcome in the Year.

Little Lamb,
Here I am;
Come and lick
My white neck;
Let me pull
Your soft Wool;
Let me kiss
Your soft face:
Merrily, Merrily, we welcome in the Year.

William Blake, 1757–1827

16

17

ANOTHER SARAH
for Christopher Smart

When winter was half over
God sent three angels to the apple-tree
Who said to her
"Be glad, you little rack
Of empty sticks,
Because you have been chosen.

In May you will become
A wave of living sweetness
A nation of white petals
A dynasty of apples."

Anne Porter, b. 1911

WE LIKE MARCH

We like March—his shoes are Purple.
He is new and high—
Makes he Mud for Dog and Peddler—
Makes he Forests Dry—
Knows the Adder's Tongue his coming
And begets her spot—
Stands the Sun so close and mighty—
That our Minds are hot.
News is he of all the others—
Bold it were to die
With the Blue Birds buccaneering
On his British sky—

Emily Dickinson, 1830–1886

March is like a long-awaited visitor who comes to town with his yearly springtime show.

I THINK

I will write you a letter,
June day. Dear June Fifth,
you're all in green, so
many kinds and all one
green, tree shadows on
grass blades and grass
blade shadows. The air
fills up with motor
mower sound. The cat
walks up the drive
a dead baby rabbit
in her maw. The sun
is hot, the breeze
is cool. And suddenly
in all the green
the lilacs bloom,
massive and exquisite
in color and shape
and scent. The roses
are more full of
buds than ever. No
flowers. But soon.
June day, you have
your own perfection:
so green to say
goodbye to. Green,
stick around
a while.

James Schuyler, b. 1923

18

SPRING

for Annie

bluebird &
honeymoon over
the house,
sun across the equator
coming higher, the earth
a quarter way round the year

things that live rise
& go after each other
in the spice
on blue wings
from austere
rot & wither

a weight is lifting
a slag of cold air.
The sun comes around the
    bend
we see him & start to cheer.

Reed Bye, b. 1948

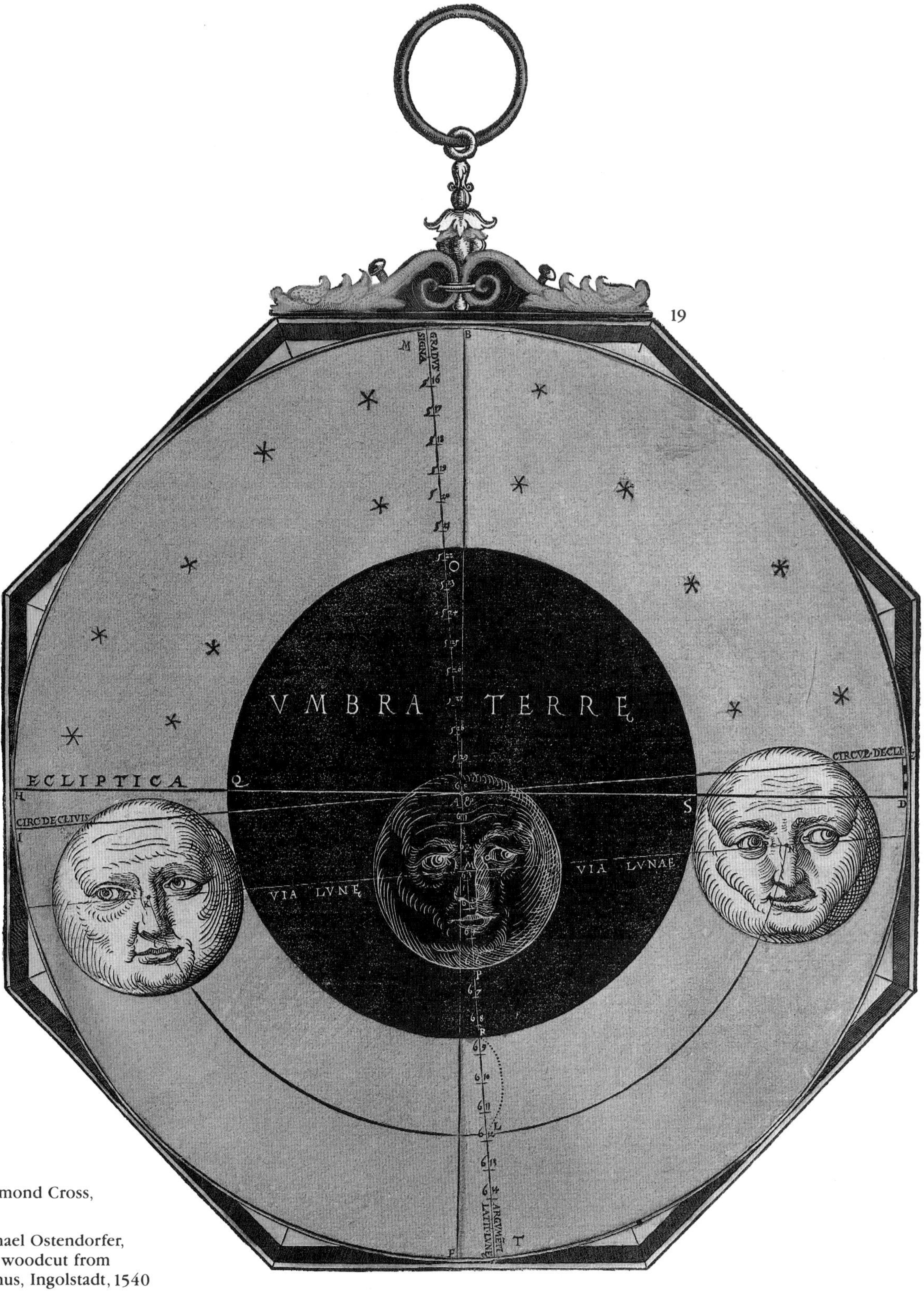

18 *The Artist's Garden at St. Clair.* Henry Edmond Cross,
    French, 1856–1910. Watercolor on paper

19 *Figura Eclipsis Plana (Total Eclipse).* Michael Ostendorfer,
    German, ca. 1519–ca. 1559. Hand-colored woodcut from
    Astronomicum caesareum by Petrus Apianus, Ingolstadt, 1540

In poetry and art, people can express the amazement and tender affection that they feel for babies and little children.

ALL THE PRETTY LITTLE HORSES

Hushaby,
Don't you cry,
Go to sleepy, little baby,
When you wake,
You shall have,
All the pretty little horses—
Blacks and bays,
Dapples and grays,
Coach and six-a little horses.
Hushaby,
Don't you cry,
Go to sleepy, little baby.
. . . .

Anonymous

LULLABY

Someone would like to have you for her child
But you are mine.
Someone would like to rear you on a costly mat
But you are mine.
Someone would like to place you on a camel blanket
But you are mine.
I have you to rear on a torn old mat.
Someone would like to have you as her child
But you are mine.

Akan people, Africa

20 *Midnight: Mother and Sleepy Child.* Kitagawa Utamaro, Japanese, 1753–1806. Colored woodblock print from the series *Customs of Women in the Twelve Hours*

21 *Danza del Venado Sonora.* Carlos Merida, Mexican, b. 1894. Colored lithograph

22 Mother and child. Wood. Irian Jaya, Sentani people, 19th–20th century

21

22

SONG OF PARENTS WHO WANT TO WAKE UP THEIR SON

Don't sleep! for your paddle fell into the water, and your spear.
Don't sleep! for the ravens and crows are flying about.

Kwakiutl Indians, North America

Puva, puva, puva,
In the trail the beetles
On each other's backs are sleeping,
So on mine, my baby, thou.
Puva, puva, puva!

Hopi Indians, North America

LULLY, LULLA

Lully, lulla, thou little tiny
  child,
By by, lully lullay.

O sisters too,
How may we do
For to preserve this day
This poor youngling,
For whom we do sing,
By by, lully lullay?

Herod, the king,
In his raging,
Charged he hath this day
His men of might,
In his own sight,
All young children to slay.

That woe is me,
Poor child for thee!
And ever morn and day,
For thy parting
Neither say nor sing
By by, lully lullay!

Lully, lulla, thou little tiny
  child,
By by, lully lullay.

Anonymous, 15th century

23

24

THE SONG OF KUK-OOK,
THE BAD BOY

This is the song of Kuk-ook, the bad boy.
    Imakayah—hayah,
    Imakayah—hay—hayah.
I am going to run away from home, *hayah,*
In a great big boat, *hayah,*
To hunt for a sweet little girl, *hayah;*
I shall get her some beads, *hayah;*
The kind that look like boiled ones, *hayah;*
Then after a while, *hayah,*

I shall come back home, *hayah,*
I shall call all my relations together, *hayah,*
And shall give them all a good thrashing, *hayah;*
I shall marry two girls at once, *hayah;*
One of the sweet little darlings, *hayah,*
I shall dress in spotted sealskins, *hayah,*
And the other dear little pet, *hayah,*
Shall wear skins of the hooded seal only, *hayah.*

Eskimo, North America

*This is the crazy daydream of a happy and rebellious
little boy.*

23 Crib of the Infant Jesus. Wood, polychromed and gilt, lead, silver gilt, painted parchment, and silk embroidered with seed pearls and translucent enamels. South Netherlandish (Brabant), 15th century

24 Shaman rattle in the form of a bird. Wood, pebbles, and paint. British Columbia (Queen Charlotte Islands), Tsimshian people, 19th century

25 *Portrait of a Young Woman.* Johannes Vermeer, Dutch, 1632–1675. Oil on canvas

25

TO MISTRESS ISABEL PENNELL

By Saint Mary, my lady,
Your mammy and your daddy
Brought forth a goodly baby!
　　My maiden Isabel,
Reflaring rosabell,
The flagrant camamell,
　　The ruddy rosary,
The sovereign rosemary,
The pretty strawberry,
　　The columbine, the nepte,
The jeloffer well set,
The proper violet;
　　Ennewèd your color
Is like the daisy flower
After the April shower;
　　Star of the morrow gray,
The blossom on the spray,
The freshest flower of May:
　　Maidenly demure,
Of womanhood the lure;
Wherefore I make you sure
　　It were an heavenly health,
It were an endless wealth,
A life for God himself,
　　To hear this nightingale
Among the birdès small
Warbling in the vale,
Dug, dug, jug, jug,
Good year and good luck,
With chuck, chuck, chuck, chuck!

　　　　　John Skelton, 1460?–1529

Isabel Pennell seems as cheery and fresh as the little flowers and bird songs of springtime. There are some old-fashioned words in this poem: reflaring *means sweet smelling,* flagrant *means blazing,* nepte *means catnip, and* jeloffer *means gillyflower.*

THE COTTAGER TO
HER INFANT

The days are cold, the nights
    are long,
The Northwind sings a
    doleful song;
Then hush again upon my
    breast;
All merry things are now at
    rest,
    Save thee, my pretty love!

The kitten sleeps upon the
    hearth;
The crickets long have ceased
    their mirth;
There's nothing stirring in
    the house

Save one wee, hungry, nibbling
    mouse,
    Then why so busy thou?

Nay! start not at the sparkling
    light;
'Tis but the moon that shines
    so bright
On the window-pane bedropped
    with rain:
There, little darling! sleep
    again,
    And wake when it is day.

Dorothy Wordsworth, 1771–1855

Minnie and Winnie are two little girls, perhaps like the little girls in this picture. The poem is probably a bedtime story, a fantasy to put the children in a dreamy, sleepy mood.

MINNIE AND WINNIE

Minnie and Winnie
    Slept in a shell.
Sleep, little ladies!
    And they slept well.

Pink was the shell within,
    Silver without;
Sounds of the great sea
    Wander'd about.

Sleep, little ladies!
    Wake not soon!
Echo on echo
    Dies to the moon.

Two bright stars
    Peep'd into the shell.
"What are they dreaming of?
    Who can tell?"

Started a green linnet
    Out of the croft;
Wake, little ladies!
    The sun is aloft!

Alfred, Lord Tennyson, 1809–1892

FROM A CHILDHOOD

The darkening was like riches in the room
in which the boy, withdrawn and secret, sat.
And when his mother entered as in a dream,
a glass quivered in the silent cabinet.
She felt how the room had given her away,
and kissed her boy: Are you here?...
Then both gazed timidly towards the piano,
for many an evening she would play a song
in which the child was strangely deeply
  caught.
He sat quite still. His big gaze hung
upon her hand which, all bowed
  down by the ring,
as it were heavily in snowdrifts going,
over the white keys went.

Rainer Maria Rilke, 1875–1926

*The moment this poem describes seems strangely
silent and vivid. It is as if time stood still, as time
can seem to stand still in a painting or in an
unforgettable memory.*

28

26 *Peasant Mother and Child*. Mary Cassatt,
   American, 1844–1926. Color etching

27 *The Calmady Children*. Sir Thomas
   Lawrence, British, 1769–1830. Oil on canvas

28 *Consuelo, Duchess of Marlborough
   (1876–1964), and Her Son, Lord Ivor
   Spencer-Churchill (1898–1956)* (detail).
   Giovanni Boldini, Italian, 1845–1931. Oil on
   canvas, 1906

SILLY SONG

Mama,
I wish I were silver.

Son,
You'd be very cold.

Mama,
I wish I were water.

Son,
You'd be very cold.

Mama,
Embroider me on your pillow.

That, yes!
Right away!

    Federico García Lorca, 1899–1936

29

30

MISS BLUES'ES CHILD

If the blues would let me,
Lord knows I would smile.
If the blues would let me,
I would smile, smile, smile.
Instead of that I'm cryin'—
I must be Miss Blues'es child.

You were my moon up in the sky,
At night my wishing star.
I love you, oh, I love you so—
But you have gone so far!

Now my days are lonely,
And night-time drives me wild.
In my heart I'm crying,
I'm just Miss Blues'es child!

    Langston Hughes, 1902–1967

29 Sampler. Millsent Connor. Silk on linen. Boston, 1799

30 *Dressing for the Carnival* (detail). Winslow Homer,
   American, 1836–1910. Oil on canvas, 1877

31 *First Steps*. Vincent van Gogh, Dutch, 1853–1890. Oil
   on canvas, 1890

KIRSTEN

you're so funny! I'd give you
   all of my money, any-
time, just to see what you'd say!
   alas, all I have is a dime.
How you talk is my heart's
   delight. You are
more terrible than your step-dad,
   more great than bright light.

Ted Berrigan, 1934–1983

*Kirsten is the step-
daughter of a friend of
the poet, Ted Berrigan.*

31

POEM FOR SHANE ON HER BROTHER'S BIRTHDAY

During the Early Winter
of 1735 The First French
String Quartets were played
like pale green snow falling
on the Golden parks of Autumn.
Birds ran and people flitted
Past bonfires of aromas
Billowing into Huge florals
of fabrics shot with
Silver and polychrome and gold
Falling around the Thighs
of The Birth of Venus

Later in the Navy Blue
Night after fireworks
Fell As Stars Tarnished
and grew cold a lilac
Gleam smelling of apples
Whizzed by in the serenity
of a Room with furniture
of Sunlight like a
Museum of Success Bearing
In Her Arms a Silver Boat
Filled like a great Basket
Filled to overflowing with
Silver Tulips of Electric Light
For her brother.

Donald T. Sanders, b. 1944

Although this poem was written for a modern little girl in New York City, it is as if the poet wanted to give her a birthday poem in which everything was extravagantly formal and old-fashioned and nothing was modern or casual or childish.

AUTOBIOGRAPHIA LITERARIA

When I was a child
I played by myself in a
corner of the schoolyard
all alone.

I hated dolls and I
hated games, animals were
not friendly and birds
flew away.

If anyone was looking
for me I hid behind a
tree and cried out "I am
an orphan."

And here I am, the
center of all beauty!
writing these poems!
Imagine!

Frank O'Hara, 1926–1966

Autobiographia Literaria *means*
literary autobiography, the
story of a writer's life.

33

32 *Still Life with Silver.* Alexandre
   François Desportes, French,
   1661–1743. Oil on canvas

33 *Soap Bubbles.* Thomas Couture,
   French, 1815–1879. Oil on canvas

31

COME LIVE WITH ME AND BE MY LOVE

Love is one of the strongest forces in people's lives, but it is hard to talk about logically. Poetry and art express things about love that couldn't otherwise be expressed.

THE PASSIONATE SHEPHERD TO HIS LOVE

Come live with me and be my love,
And we will all the pleasures prove
That valleys, groves, hills, and fields,
Woods, or steepy mountain yields.

And we will sit upon the rocks,
Seeing the shepherds feed their flocks,
By shallow rivers to whose falls
Melodious birds sing madrigals.

And I will make thee beds of roses
And a thousand fragrant posies,
A cap of flowers, and a kirtle
Embroidered all with leaves of myrtle;

A gown made of the finest wool
Which from our pretty lambs we pull;
Fair-lined slippers for the cold,
With buckles of the purest gold;

A belt of straw and ivy buds,
With coral clasps and amber studs:
And if these pleasures may thee move,
Come live with me, and be my love.

The shepherds' swains shall dance and sing
For thy delight each May morning:
If these delights thy mind may move,
Then live with me and be my love.

Christopher Marlowe, 1564–1593

34 Detail of an embroidery. English, 17th century

35 *Bahram Gur with the Indian Princess in Her Black Pavilion.* Leaf from a *Haft Paykar* by Nizami. Ink, color, and gold on paper. Herat, Timurid School, ca. 1426

35

ALTHOUGH I CONQUER ALL THE EARTH

Although I conquer all the earth,
Yet for me there is only one city.
In that city there is for me only one house;
And in that house, one room only;
And in that room, a bed.
And one woman sleeps there,
The shining joy and jewel of all my kingdom.

Ancient India

33

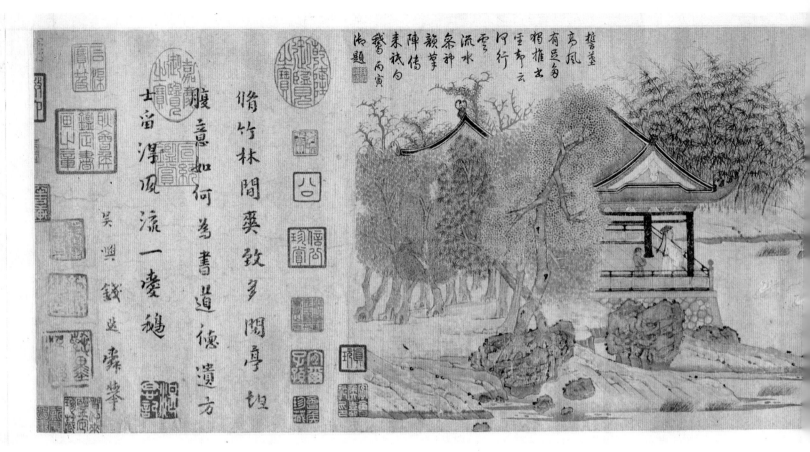

THE RIVER-MERCHANT'S WIFE: A LETTER

While my hair was still cut straight across my forehead
I played about the front gate, pulling flowers.
You came by on bamboo stilts, playing horse,
You walked about my seat, playing with blue plums.
And we went on living in the village of Chōkan:
Two small people, without dislike or suspicion.

At fourteen I married My Lord you.
I never laughed, being bashful.
Lowering my head, I looked at the wall.
Called to, a thousand times, I never looked back.

At fifteen I stopped scowling,
I desired my dust to be mingled with yours
Forever and forever and forever.
Why should I climb the lookout?

At sixteen you departed,
You went into far Ku-tō-en, by the river of swirling
    eddies,
And you have been gone five months.
The monkeys make sorrowful noise overhead.

You dragged your feet when you went out.
By the gate now, the moss is grown, the different mosses,
Too deep to clear them away!
The leaves fall early this autumn, in wind.
The paired butterflies are already yellow with August
Over the grass in the West garden;
They hurt me. I grow older.
If you are coming down through the narrows of the river
    Kiang,
Please let me know beforehand,
And I will come out to meet you
        As far as Chō-fū-Sa.

Ezra Pound, 1885–1972, after Li Po, A.D. 705–762

This poem is a letter of devoted love and longing from a lonely young wife to her husband, a river merchant, who has been away from home for a long time.

36 *Wang Hsi-chih Watching Geese.*
Ch'ien Hsüan, Chinese,
ca. 1235–1300. Handscroll, ink,
color, and gold on paper

37 *The Steward Memi-Sabu and
His Wife.* Painted limestone.
Egyptian, Dynasty 5, ca. 2360 B.C.

37

OATH OF FRIENDSHIP

Shang ya!
I want to be your friend
For ever and ever without break or decay.
When the hills are all flat
And the rivers are all dry,
When it lightens and thunders in winter,
When it rains and snows in summer,
When Heaven and Earth mingle—
Not till then will I part from you.

Anonymous, China, 1st century B.C.

SONNET

Guido, I wish that you and Lapo and I
Were carried off by magic
And put in a boat, which, every time there was wind,
Would sail on the ocean exactly where we wanted.

In this way storms and other dangerous weather
Wouldn't be able to harm us—
And I wish that, since we all were of one mind,
We would want more and more to be together.

And I wish that Vanna and Lagia too
And the girl whose name on the list is number thirty
Were put in the boat by the magician too

And that we all did nothing but talk about love
And I wish that they were just as glad to be there
As I believe the three of us would be.

Dante Alighieri, 1265–1321

38

36

39

PHILLIDA AND CORIDON

In the merry month of May,
In a morn by break of day
Forth I walked by the wood-side,
Whenas May was in his pride.
There I spièd, all alone,
Phillida and Coridon.
Much ado there was, God wot,
He would love and she would not.
She said, Never man was true;
He said, None was false to you.
He said he had loved her long.
She said, Love should have no wrong.
Coridon would kiss her then;
She said maids must kiss no men
Till they did for good and all.

Then she made the shepherd call
All the heavens to witness truth,
Never loved a truer youth.
Thus, with many a pretty oath,
Yea and nay, and faith and troth,
Such as silly shepherds use
When they will not love abuse,
Love which had been long deluded
Was with kisses sweet concluded.
And Phillida with garlands gay
Was made the lady of the May.

Nicholas Breton, 1551?–ca. 1623

By the end of this poem Coridon has persuaded Phillida to kiss him.

38 *Boating*. Edouard Manet, French,
　1832–1883. Oil on canvas, 1874

39 *The Stolen Kiss*. Jean Honoré
　Fragonard, French, 1732–1806.
　Oil on canvas

IT WAS A LOVER AND HIS LASS

It was a lover, and his lass,
    With a hey, and a ho, and a hey nonino,
That o'er the green cornfield did pass,
    In spring time, the only pretty ring time,
When birds do sing, hey ding a ding, ding:
Sweet lovers love the spring.

Between the acres of the rye
    With a hey, and a ho, and a hey nonino,
These pretty country folks would lie,
    In spring time, the only pretty ring time,
When birds do sing, hey ding a ding, ding:
Sweet lovers love the spring.

This carol they began that hour,
    With a hey, and a ho, and a hey nonino;
How that a life was but a flower,
    In spring time, the only pretty ring time,
When birds do sing, hey ding a ding, ding;
Sweet lovers love the spring.

And therefore take the present time,
    With a hey, and a ho, and a hey nonino;
For love is crownèd with the prime
    In spring time, the only pretty ring time,
When birds do sing, hey ding a ding, ding:
Sweet lovers love the spring.

William Shakespeare, 1564–1616

40

40 *The Fair at Bezons*
(detail). Jean Baptiste
Joseph Pater, French,
1695–1736. Oil on canvas

41 *Paradise* (detail).
Giovanni di Paolo, Italian
(Sienese), 1403?–1482/83.
Tempera and gold on
canvas, transferred
from wood

41

UPON JULIA'S CLOTHES

Whenas in silks my Julia goes,
Then, then, me thinks,
    how sweetly flows
That liquefaction of her clothes.

Next, when I cast mine eyes and see
That brave vibration each way free,
O how that glittering taketh me!

Robert Herrick

A TERNARY OF LITTLES, UPON A PIPKIN OF JELLY SENT TO A LADY

A little saint best fits a little shrine,
A little prop best fits a little vine,
As my small cruse best fits my little wine.

A little seed best fits a little soil,
A little trade best fits a little toil:
As my small jar best fits my little oil.

A little bin best fits a little bread,
A little garland fits a little head:
As my small stuff best fits my little shed.

A little hearth best fits a little fire,
A little chapel fits a little choir,
As my small bell best fits my little spire.

A little stream best fits a little boat;
A little lead best fits a little float;
As my small pipe best fits my little note.

A little meat best fits a little belly,
As sweetly lady, give me leave to tell ye
This little pipkin fits this little jelly.

                    Robert Herrick, 1591–1674

*A ternary is a trio or group of three, like the three lines in each of these stanzas.
A cruse is a cup or glass, a pipkin is a little pot.*

43

I HAVE LIVED AND I HAVE LOVED

I have lived and I have loved;
I have waked and I have slept;
I have sung and I have danced;
I have smiled and I have wept;
I have won and wasted
    treasure;
I have had my fill of pleasure;
And all these things were
    weariness,
And some of them were
    dreariness.
And all these things—but
    two things
Were emptiness and pain:
And Love—it was the best
    of them;
And Sleep—worth all the rest
    of them.

                    Anonymous

42 Reliquary shrine of the Virgin and
Child. Believed to have been made
for Queen Elizabeth of Hungary.
Silver-gilt and translucent enamel.
French (Paris), ca. 1340–50

43 Sundial. Paul Reinman, German
(Nuremberg), 1575–1609. One panel
of a diptych, ivory

42

39

GREENSLEEVES

Greensleeves was all my joy,
    Greensleeves was my delight;
Greensleeves was my heart of gold,
    And who but Lady Greensleeves?

Alas, my love, you do me wrong
    To cast me off discourteously;
And I have lovéd you so long,
    Delighting in your company.

I have been ready at your hand
    To grant whatever you would crave;
I have both wagéd life and land,
    Your love and good will for to have.

I bought thee kerchiefs to thy head,
    That were wrought fine and gallantly;
I kept thee both at board and bed,
    Which cost my purse well favoredly.

I bought thee petticoats of the best,
    The cloth so fine as fine might be;
I gave thee jewels for thy chest,
    And all this cost I spent on thee.

Thy smock of silk both fair and white,
    With gold embroidered gorgeously;
Thy petticoat of sendal right,
    And thus I bought thee gladly.

Thy girdle of gold so red,
    With pearls bedeckèd sumptuously,
The like no other lasses had,
    And yet thou wouldst not love me.

. . . .

Thy crimson stockings all of silk,
    With gold all wrought above the knee,
Thy pumps as white as was the milk,
    And yet thou wouldst not love me.

Thy gown was of the grossy green,
    Thy sleeves of satin hanging by,
Which made thee be our harvest queen
    And yet thou wouldst not love me.

. . . .

Greensleeves was all my joy,
    Greensleeves was my delight;
Greensleeves was my heart of gold,
    And who but Lady Greensleeves?

                  Anonymous, 18th century

In the sixth stanza, sendal *is a kind of silk.*

44 Two pairs of dancers. Models by Joseph Nees, German (Ludwigsburg), active 1759–68. Hard-paste porcelain, ca. 1760–63

45 *Rudabeh Makes a Ladder of Her Tresses.* Attributed to Qadimi. Detail of a leaf of the *Shah-nameh* made for Shah Tahmasp. Colors, ink, silver, and gold on paper. Safavid period, ca. 1525

46 Woodcut, Sumi-ye, from a set of twelve sheets. Hishikawa Moronobu, Japanese, ca. 1625–1694

44

45

A BIRTHDAY

My heart is like a singing bird
    Whose nest is in a watered shoot;
My heart is like an apple-tree
    Whose boughs are bent with thickset fruit;
My heart is like a rainbow shell
    That paddles in a halcyon sea;
My heart is gladder than all these
    Because my love is come to me.

Raise me a dais of silk and down;
    Hang it with vair and purple dyes;
Carve it in doves and pomegranates,
    And peacocks with a hundred eyes;
Work it in gold and silver grapes,
    In leaves and silver fleurs-de-lys;
Because the birthday of my life
    Is come, my love is come to me.

Christina Rossetti, 1830–1894

Vair, *in the second stanza, is a kind of fur.*

46

INDIAN SERENADE

I arise from dreams of thee
In the first sweet sleep of night,
When the winds are breathing low,
And the stars are shining bright:
I arise from dreams of thee,
And a spirit in my feet
Has led me—who knows how?
To thy chamber window, Sweet!

The wandering airs they faint
On the dark, the silent stream—
The Champak odours fail
Like sweet thoughts in a dream;

The nightingale's complaint,
It dies upon her heart;—
As I must die on thine,
Belovèd as thou art!

O lift me from the grass!
I die, I faint, I fail!
Let thy love in kisses rain
On my lips and eyelids pale.
My cheek is cold and white, alas!
My heart beats loud and fast;—
Oh! press it close to thine again,
Where it will break at last.

Percy Bysshe Shelley, 1792–1822

Champak, *in the second stanza, is an Indian tree with fragrant flowers.*

TO AN ISLE IN THE WATER

Shy one, shy one,
Shy one of my heart,
She moves in the firelight
Pensively apart.

She carries in the dishes,
And lays them in a row.
To an isle in the water
With her would I go.

She carries in the candles,
And lights the curtained room,
Shy in the doorway
And shy in the gloom;

And shy as a rabbit,
Helpful and shy.
To an isle in the water
With her would I fly.

William Butler Yeats, 1865–1939

47

42

THE LETTER

Where is another sweet as my sweet,
    Fine of the fine, and shy of the shy?
Fine little hands, fine little feet—
    Dewy blue eye.
Shall I write to her? shall I go?
    Ask her to marry me by and by?
Somebody said that she'd say no;
    Somebody knows that she'll say ay!

Ay or no, if ask'd to her face?
    Ay or no, from shy of the shy?
Go, little letter, apace, apace,
      Fly;
Fly to the light in the valley below—
    Tell my wish to her dewy blue eye.
Somebody said that she'd say no;
    Somebody knows that she'll say ay!

Alfred, Lord Tennyson, 1809–1892

48

47 *The Proposal*. Adolphe William Bouguereau,
   French, 1825–1905. Oil on canvas, 1872

48 *The Love Letter*. Jean Honoré Fragonard,
   French, 1732–1806. Oil on canvas

OH, WHEN I WAS IN LOVE WITH YOU

Oh, when I was in love with you,
    Then I was clean and brave,
And miles around the wonder grew
    How well did I behave.

And now the fancy passes by,
    And nothing will remain,
And miles around they'll say that I
    Am quite myself again.

A. E. Housman, 1859–1936

49

50

HOPS

Beneath the willow, wound round with ivy,
We take cover from the worst
Of the storm, with a greatcoat round
Our shoulders and my hands around your waist.

I've got it wrong. That isn't ivy
Entwined in the bushes round
The wood, but hops. You intoxicate me!
Let's spread the greatcoat on the ground.

Boris Pasternak, 1890–1960

I WANT TO SAY YOUR NAME

I want to say your name, Naëtt! I want to make you an
    incantation, Naëtt!

Naëtt, her name has the sweetness of cinnamon it's the perfume
    where the wood of lemon trees sleeps.
Naëtt, her name has the sugared whiteness of coffee trees in flower
It's the savannah which blazes beneath the masculine love of
    the mid-day sun.
Name of dew cooler than shade and the tamarind tree
Cooler than the quickly-passing dusk when the heat of day
    is silenced.

Naëtt, it's the dry whirlwind and the dense clap of thunder.

Naëtt coin of gold coal of light my night and my sun
I your champion I have made myself a sorcerer to name you
Princess of Elissa exiled from Fouta on a catastrophic day.

Léopold Sédar Senghor, b. 1906

*Just a beautiful fragment, like the one pictured here, can suggest the
living presence of the woman who inspired it. In this poem, just the name
of the woman he loves suggests to the poet the excitement and passion he
feels when he is with her.*

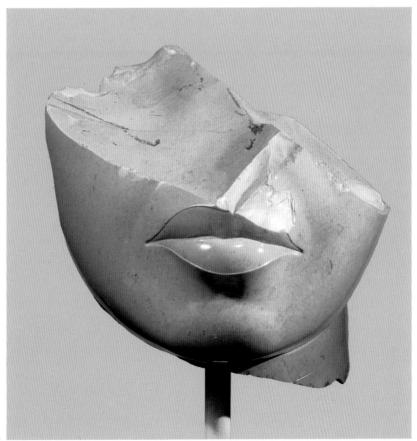

51

49 *Mezzetin*. Jean Antoine
Watteau, French, 1684–1721.
Oil on canvas

50 *The Storm*. Pierre Auguste
Cot, French, 1837–1883. Oil
on canvas, 1880

51 Fragment of a head of Queen
Tiye. Yellow jasper. Egyptian,
Dynasty 18, ca. 1417–1379 B.C.

52

SUNDAY

The mint bed is in
bloom: lavender haze
day. The grass is
more than green and
throws up sharp and
cutting lights to
slice through the
plane tree leaves. And
on the cloudless blue
I scribble your name.

James Schuyler, b. 1923

53

JUKE BOX LOVE SONG

I could take the Harlem night
and wrap around you,
Take the neon lights and make a crown,
Take the Lenox Avenue busses,
Taxis, subways,
And for your love song tone their rumble down.
Take Harlem's heartbeat,
Make a drumbeat,
Put it on a record, let it whirl,
And while we listen to it play,
Dance with you till day—
Dance with you, my sweet brown Harlem girl.

Langston Hughes, 1902–1967

54

SONG

Did you see me walking by the Buick Repairs?
I was thinking of you
having a Coke in the heat it was your face
I saw on the movie magazine, no it was Fabian's
I was thinking of you
and down at the railroad tracks where the station
has mysteriously disappeared
I was thinking of you
as the bus pulled away in the twilight
I was thinking of you
and right now

Frank O'Hara, 1926–1966

52 *Arques-la-Bataille*. John H. Twachtman,
   American, 1853–1902. Oil on canvas, 1885

53 *New York City at Night*. Berenice Abbott,
   American, b. 1898. Gelatin silver photograph,
   1933

54 *Le Coeur*. Henri Matisse, French, 1869–1954.
   Pochoir from *Jazz*. Paris, Tériade, 1947

What seems to be nonsense sometimes makes a strange kind of sense. Poetry can be funny, nonsensical, and true all at the same time.

WHEN THE GREEN WOODS LAUGH

When the green woods laugh with
   the voice of joy,
And the dimpling stream runs
   laughing by,
When the air does laugh with our
   merry wit,
And the green hill laughs with the
   noise of it.

When the meadows laugh with lively
   green,
And the grasshopper laughs in the
   merry scene,
When Mary and Susan and Emily
With their sweet round mouths sing
   "Ha, Ha, He!"

When the painted birds laugh in the
   shade,
Where our table with cherries and
   nuts is spread,
Come live & be merry, and join
   with me,
To sing the sweet chorus of
   "Ha, Ha, He!"

William Blake, 1757–1827

55

48

THE KOOCOO

In April, the koocoo can sing her song by rote,
In June—of tune—she cannot sing a note;
At first, *koo-coo, koo-coo,* sing still can she do,
At last, *kooke, kooke, kooke;* six *kookes* to one *koo.*

Anonymous, 16th century

56

IF ALL THE WORLD WERE PAPER

If all the world were paper,
And all the sea were ink;
If all the trees were bread and cheese,
How should we do for drink?

If all the world were sand-o,
Oh, then what should we lack-o?
If as they say, there were no clay,
How should we take tobacco?

If all our vessels ran-a,
If none but had a crack-a;
If Spanish apes eat all the grapes,
How should we do for sack-a?

If friars had no bald pates,
Nor nuns had no dark cloisters;
If all the seas were beans and peas,
How should we do for oysters?

If there had been no projects,
Nor none that did great wrongs;
If fiddlers shall turn players all,
How should we do for songs?

If all things were eternal,
And nothing their end bringing;
If this should be, then how should we
Here make an end of singing?

Anonymous, 17th century

49

A NUT TREE

I had a little nut tree,
    Nothing would it bear,
But a silver nutmeg,
    And a golden pear.
The King of Spain's daughter
    Came to visit me,
And all was because of
    My little nut tree.
I skipped over water
    I danced over sea,
And all the birds in the air
    Could not catch me.

Anonymous

Sometimes the only purpose of a poem is to be light, fun, and fanciful.

58

57

MEET-ON-THE-ROAD

"Now, pray, where are you going, child?" said Meet-on-the-Road.
"To school, sir, to school, sir," said Child-as-It-Stood.

"What have you in your basket, child?" said Meet-on-the-Road.
"My dinner, sir, my dinner, sir," said Child-as-It-Stood.

"What have you for your dinner, child?" said Meet-on-the-Road.
"Some pudding, sir, some pudding, sir," said Child-as-It-Stood.

"Oh, then I pray, give me a share," said Meet-on-the-Road.
"I've little enough for myself, sir," said Child-as-It-Stood.

"What have you got that cloak on for?" said Meet-on-the-Road.
"To keep the wind and cold from me," said Child-as-It-Stood.

"I wish the wind would blow through you," said Meet-on-the-Road.
"Oh, what a wish! Oh, what a wish!" said Child-as-It-Stood.

"Pray what are those bells ringing for?" said Meet-on-the-Road.
"To ring bad spirits home again," said Child-as-It-Stood.

"Oh, then, I must be going, child," said Meet-on-the-Road.
"So fare you well, so fare you well," said Child-as-It-Stood.

Anonymous

57 Automaton in the form of a chariot pushed by a Chinese attendant and set with a clock. James Cox, d. 1791. Gold, brilliants, and paste jewels. London, 1766

58 *Grainfields* (detail). Jacob Isaacksz. van Ruisdael, Dutch, 1628/9–1682. Oil on canvas

59 *Scenes from the Story of the Argonauts* (detail). Workshop of Biagio di Antonio, Italian (Florentine), active 1476–1504. Tempera on wood, gilt ornaments

60 *Tête à tête am Wolkenkratzer 968 étage.* Moriz Jung, Austrian, 1885–1915. Color lithograph. Vienna, the Wiener Werkstätte

BINGO

The miller's mill-dog lay at the mill-door,
And his name was Little Bingo.
B with an I, I with an N, N with a G, G with an O,
And his name was Little Bingo.

The miller he bought a cask of ale,
And he called it right good Stingo.
S with a T, T with an I, I with an N, N with a G, G with an O,
And he called it right good Stingo.

The miller he went to town one day,
And he bought a wedding Ring-o!
R with an I, I with an N, N with a G, G with an O,
And he bought a wedding Ring-o!

Anonymous

59

60

I'LL SAIL UPON THE DOG-STAR

I'll sail upon the Dog-star,
And then pursue the morning;
I'll chase the Moon till it be noon,
But I'll make her leave her horning.

I'll climb the frosty mountain,
And there I'll coin the weather;
I'll tear the rainbow from the sky
And tie both ends together.

The stars pluck from their orbs too,
And crowd them in my budget;
And whether I'm a roaring boy,
Let all the nation judge it.

Thomas Durfey, 1653–1723

HUMPTY DUMPTY'S RECITATION

In winter, when the fields are white,
I sing this song for your delight—

In spring, when woods are getting
green,
I'll try and tell you what I mean.

In summer, when the days are long,
Perhaps you'll understand the song.

In autumn, when the leaves are brown,
Take pen and ink and write it down.

I sent a message to the fish:
I told them "This is what I wish."

The little fishes of the sea
They sent an answer back to me.

The little fishes' answer was
"We cannot do it, Sir, because—"

I sent to them again to say
"It will be better to obey."

The fishes answered with a grin,
"Why, what a temper you are in!"

I told them once, I told them twice:
They would not listen to advice.

I took a kettle large and new,
Fit for the deed I had to do.

My heart went hop, my heart went
thump;
I filled the kettle at the pump.

Then someone came to me and said
"The little fishes are in bed."

I said to him, I said it plain,
"Then you must wake them up again."

I said it loud and very clear;
I went and shouted in his ear.

But he was very stiff and proud;
He said "You needn't shout so loud!"

And he was very proud and stiff;
He said "I'll go and wake them, if—"

I took a corkscrew from the shelf:
I went to wake them up myself.

And when I found the door was locked,
I pulled and pushed and kicked and
knocked.

And when I found the door was shut,
I tried to turn the handle, but—

Lewis Carroll, 1832–1898

61

52

62

JABBERWOCKY

'Twas brillig, and the slithy toves
    Did gyre and gimble in the wabe;
All mimsy were the borogroves,
    And the mome raths outgrabe.

"Beware the Jabberwock, my son!
    The jaws that bite, the claws that catch!
Beware the Jubjub bird, and shun
    The frumious Bandersnatch!"

He took his vorpal sword in hand:
    Long time the manxome foe he sought—
So rested he by the Tumtum tree,
    And stood awhile in thought.

And as in uffish thought he stood,
    The Jabberwock, with eyes of flame,
Came whiffling through the tulgey wood,
    And burbled as it came!

One, two! One, two! And through and through
    The vorpal blade went snicker-snack!
He left it dead, and with its head
    He came galumphing back.

"And hast thou slain the Jabberwock?
    Come to my arms, my beamish boy!
O frabjous day! Callooh! Callay!"
    He chortled in his joy.

'Twas brillig, and the slithy toves
    Did gyre and gimble in the wabe;
All mimsy were the borogroves,
    And the mome raths outgrabe.

Lewis Carroll

THE BIG ROCK CANDY MOUNTAINS

One evening as the sun went down
And the jungle fire was burning,
Down the track came a hobo hiking.
And he said, "Boys I'm not turning,
I'm headed for a land that's far away,
Beside the crystal fountains,
So come with me, we'll go and see
The Big Rock Candy Mountains."

In the Big Rock Candy Mountains,
There's land that's fair and bright,
Where the handouts grow on bushes,
And you sleep out every night.
Where the boxcars are all empty,
And the sun shines every day
On the birds and the bees,
And the cigarette trees,
And the lemonade springs
Where the bluebird sings
In the Big Rock Candy Mountains.

. . . .

American folksong, 19th–20th century

61 *Michigan Boulevard with Mayor Daley.* Red Grooms,
   American, b. 1937. Watercolor and collage, 1969

62 Detail of an imperial dragon robe, silk embroidered with
   silks, seed pearls, silver, and gold threads. Chinese, late
   18th–early 19th century

THE OWL AND THE PUSSY-CAT

The Owl and the Pussy-cat went to sea
    In a beautiful pea-green boat,
They took some honey, and plenty of
    money,
    Wrapped up in a five-pound note.
The Owl looked up to the stars above,
    And sang to a small guitar,
"O lovely Pussy! O Pussy, my love,
    What a beautiful Pussy you are,
       You are,
       You are!
    What a beautiful Pussy you are!"

Pussy said to the Owl, "You elegant fowl!
    How charmingly sweet you sing!
O let us be married! too long we have
    tarried:
    But what shall we do for a ring?"
They sailed away, for a year and a day,
    To the land where the Bong-Tree
    grows,
And there in a wood a Piggy-wig stood,
    With a ring at the end of his nose,
       His nose,
       His nose,
    With a ring at the end of his nose.

"Dear Pig, are you willing to sell for
    one shilling
    Your ring?" Said the Piggy, "I will."
So they took it away, and were married
    next day
    By the Turkey who lives on the hill.
They dined on mince, and slices of
    quince,
    Which they ate with a runcible spoon;
And hand in hand, on the edge of the
    sand,
    They danced by the light of the moon,
       The moon,
       The moon,
    They danced by the light of the moon.

            Edward Lear, 1812–1888

A silly-seeming poem can inspire a serious feeling, like the desire to sail far, far away.

63

While your outer self looks ordinary, your inner self can be a constantly changing kaleidoscope of who you are, what you know, and what you have the power, perhaps, to know and to be.

64

"I AM CHERRY ALIVE," THE LITTLE GIRL SANG

For Miss Kathleen Hanlon

"I am cherry alive," the little girl sang,
"Each morning I am something new:
I am apple, I am plum, I am just as excited
As the boys who made the Hallowe'en bang:
I am tree, I am cat, I am blossom too:
When I like, if I like, I can be someone new,
Someone very old, a witch in a zoo:
I can be someone else whenever I think who,
And I want to be everything sometimes too:
And the peach has a pit and I know that too,
And I put it in along with everything
To make the grown-ups laugh whenever I sing:
And I sing: *It is true; It is untrue;*
I know, I know, the true is untrue,
The peach has a pit, the pit has a peach:
And both may be wrong when I sing my song,
But I don't tell the grown-ups: because it is sad,
And I want them to laugh just like I do
Because they grew up and forgot what they
    knew
And they are sure I will forget it some day too.
They are wrong. They are wrong. When I
    sang my song, I knew, I knew!
I am red, I am gold, I am green, I am blue,
I will always be me, I will always be new!"

            Delmore Schwartz, 1913–1966

COUNTING-OUT RHYME

Silver bark of beech, and sallow
Bark of yellow birch and yellow
   Twig of willow.

Stripe of green in moosewood
   maple,
Color seen in leaf of apple,
   Bark of popple.

Wood of popple pale as
   moonbeam,
Wood of oak for yoke and
   barn-beam,
   Wood of hornbeam.

Silver bark of beech, and hollow
Stem of elder, tall and yellow
   Twig of willow.

      Edna St. Vincent Millay, 1892–1950

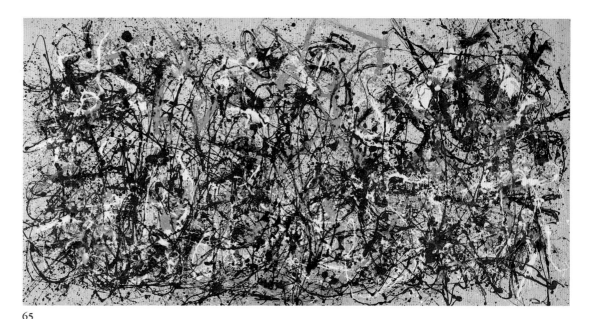

65

66

TODAY

Oh! kangaroos, sequins, chocolate sodas!
You really are beautiful! Pearls,
harmonicas, jujubes, aspirins! all
the stuff they've always talked about

still makes a poem a surprise!
These things are with us every day
even on beachheads and biers. They
do have meaning. They're strong as rocks.

      Frank O'Hara, 1926–1966

Bright, strong words can make a poem surprising, as bright, strong colors can make a painting surprising.

63 *Lake George, Free Study.* John Frederick Kensett, American, 1816–1872. Oil on canvas

64 Detail of a handscroll, ink and color on paper. Japanese, Ukiyo-e School, 18th–19th century

65 *Autumn Rhythm.* Jackson Pollock, American, 1912–1956. Oil on canvas, 1950

66 *Magic Box.* Kenneth Noland, American, b. 1924. Acrylic on canvas, 1959

Animals, who are so much a part of our world but who at the same time live in mysterious worlds of their own, have fascinated and inspired poets and artists.

67

A RABBIT AS KING OF THE GHOSTS

The difficulty to think at the end of day,
When the shapeless shadow covers the sun
And nothing is left except light on your fur—

There was the cat slopping its milk all day,
Fat cat, red tongue, green mind, white milk
And August the most peaceful month.

To be, in the grass, in the peacefullest time,
Without that monument of cat,
The cat forgotten in the moon;

And to feel that the light is a rabbit-light,
In which everything is meant for you
And nothing need be explained;

Then there is nothing to think of. It comes
of itself;

And east rushes west and west rushes down,
No matter. The grass is full

And full of yourself. The trees around are
for you,
The whole of the wideness of night is for you,
A self that touches all edges,

You become a self that fills the four corners
of night.
The red cat hides away in the fur-light
And there you are humped high, humped up,

You are humped higher and higher, black
as stone—
You sit with your head like a carving in space
And the little green cat is a bug in the grass.

Wallace Stevens, 1879–1955

56

THE MAGNIFICENT BULL

My bull is white like the silver fish in the river
White like the shimmering crane bird on the river bank
White like fresh milk!
His roar is like the thunder to the Turkish cannon on the
    steep shore.
My bull is dark like the raincloud in the storm.
He is like summer and winter
Half of him is dark like the storm cloud,
Half of him is light like sunshine.
His back shines like the morning star.
His brow is red like the beak of the hornbill.
His forehead is like a flag, calling the people from a
    distance,
He resembles the rainbow.

I will water him at the river,
With my spear I shall drive my enemies.
Let them water their herds at the well;
The river belongs to me and my bull.
Drink, my bull, from the river; I am here
To guard you with my spear.

                          Dinka people, Africa

GROUND-SQUIRREL SONG

The squirrel in his shirt
   stands up there,
The squirrel in his shirt
   stands up there;
Slender, he stands up there;
   striped, he stands up there.

             Navaho Indians,
             North America

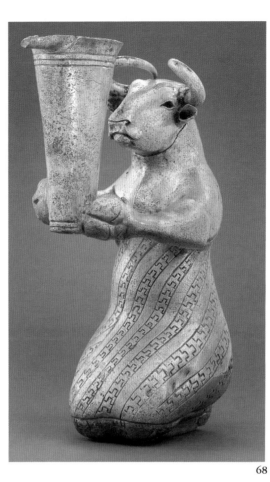

68

I SING FOR THE ANIMALS

Out of the earth
I sing for them,
A Horse nation
I sing for them.
Out of the earth
I sing for them,
The animals
I sing for them.

Teton Sioux Indians,
North America

69

67 Detail of a woodblock print,
   Surimono. Kubo Shunman,
   Japanese, 1757–1820

68 Kneeling bull holding vessel.
   Silver. Southwest Iran,
   Proto-Elamite period, ca. 2900 B.C.

69 Album leaf. Katsushika Hokusai,
   Japanese, 1760–1849. Ink and
   colors on paper

70 Detail of a tunic, feathers sewn to
   cotton fabric. Peruvian (South
   Coast), 11th–13th century

70

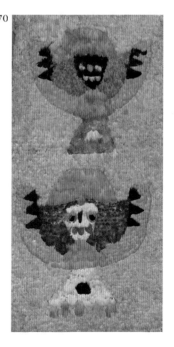

THE WAR GOD'S HORSE SONG

I am the Turquoise Woman's son

On top of Belted Mountain beautiful horses
Slim like a weasel

My horse has a hoof like striped agate
His fetlock is like fine eagle plume
His legs are like quick lightning

My horse's body is like an eagle-feathered arrow

My horse has a tail like a trailing black cloud

I put flexible goods on my horse's back

The Holy Wind blows through his mane
His mane is made of rainbows

My horse's ears are made of round corn

My horse's eyes are made of stars

My horse's head is made of mixed waters
   (from the holy waters)
   (he never knows thirst)

My horse's teeth are made of white shell

The long rainbow is in his mouth for a
   bridle
With it I guide him

When my horse neighs
Different-colored horses follow

When my horse neighs
Different-colored sheep follow

I am wealthy from my horse

Before me peaceful
Behind me peaceful
Under me peaceful
Over me peaceful
Around me peaceful
Peaceful voice when he neighs
I am everlasting and peaceful
I stand for my horse

Navaho Indians, North America

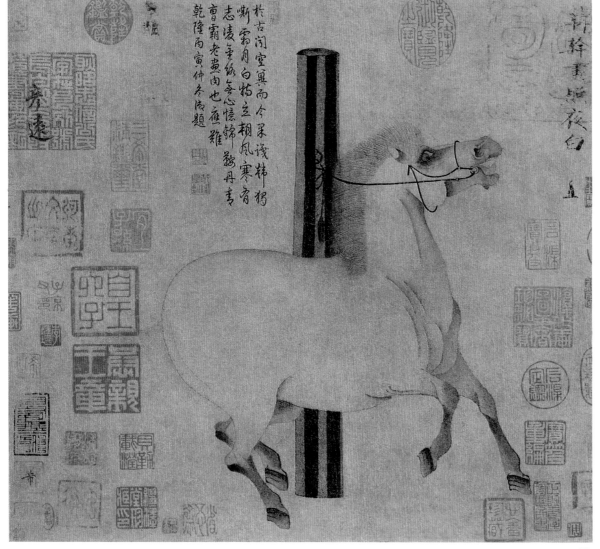

71 *Night-Shining White.* Han Kan,
   Chinese, active ca. A.D. 742–756.
   Detail of a leaf of a handscroll,
   ink on paper

72 *Unicorns (Legend—Sea Calm)*
   (detail). Arthur B. Davies,
   American, 1862–1928. Oil on
   canvas, ca. 1906

73 *From My Studio Window* (detail).
   John Kane, American, 1860–1934.
   Oil on canvas, 1932

74 Tile with an equestrian figure.
   Composite body, painted and
   glazed. Persian, second half of the
   19th century

71

I STOOD IN THE MAYTIME MEADOWS

I stood in the Maytime
    meadows
        By roses circled round
Where many a fragile blossom
        Was bright upon the ground;
And as though the roses
    called them
        And their wild hearts
understood,
The little birds were singing
        In the shadows of the wood.
The nightingale among them
        Sang sweet and loud and
long,
Until a greater voice than hers
        Rang out above her song.

For suddenly between the
    crags,

Along a narrow vale
The echoes of a hunting horn
        Came clear along the gale.
The hunter stood beside me
        Who blew that mighty horn,
I saw that he was hunting
        The noble unicorn.

The unicorn is noble;
        He keeps him safe and high
Upon a narrow path and steep
        Climbing to the sky;
And there no man can take him;
        He scorns the hunter's dart
And only a virgin's magic power
        Shall tame his haughty heart.

Anonymous, medieval

72

From THE UNICORN

Oh this is the animal that never was.
They hadn't seen one; but just the same, they loved
its graceful movements, and the way it stood
looking at them calmly, with clear eyes. . . .
. . . .

Rainer Maria Rilke, 1875–1926

TO RIDE

The street is soon there,
On the street the horse.

More beautiful than the crow
He needs a path.

Slender leg, nimble hero
Who follows his master
    toward repose.

The street is soon there
You run, you march, you trot
And then you stop.

Paul Eluard, 1895–1952

73

74

THE WHITE HORSE

The youth walks up to the white horse, to put its halter on
and the horse looks at him in silence.
They are so silent they are in another world.

D. H. Lawrence, 1885–1930

ENGRAVED ON THE COLLAR OF A DOG, WHICH I GAVE TO HIS ROYAL HIGHNESS

I am his Highness' dog at Kew;
Pray tell me, sir, whose dog are you?

Alexander Pope, 1688–1744

76

The odd punctuation makes these lines seem to move with the suddenness and quickness of a little mouse who is always hiding, darting about, and unexpectedly reappearing.

here's a little mouse

here's a little mouse) and
what does he think about, i
wonder as over this
floor (quietly with

bright eyes) drifts (nobody
can tell because
Nobody knows, or why
jerks Here &, here,
gr(oo)ving the room's Silence) this like
a littlest
poem a
(with wee ears and see?

tail frisks)
                    (gonE)
"mouse",
          We are not the same you and

i, since here's a little he
or is
it It
? (or was something we saw in the mirror)?

therefore we'll kiss;for maybe
what was Disappeared
into ourselves
who   (look).   ,startled

e. e. cummings, 1894–1962

75

60

75 *James Stuart (1612–1655), Duke of Richmond and Lennox* (detail). Anthony van Dyck, Flemish, 1599–1641. Oil on canvas

76 Snuffbox in the form of a rat. Hard-paste porcelain with contemporaneous gold mounts. Meissen, ca. 1745

77 Detail of one of a pair of six-fold screens. Suizan Miki, Japanese, 1891–1957. Ink on silvered paper

78 *The Tyger* (detail). William Blake, British, 1757–1827. Relief engraving printed in color for *Songs of Innocence and Experience*

79 *Deer in the Moonlight.* William Morris Hunt, American, 1824–1879. Lithograph, 1859

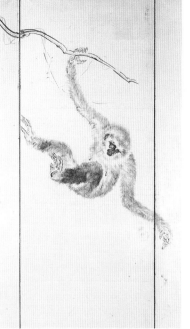

77

AUTUMN COVE

At Autumn Cove, so many white monkeys,
bounding, leaping up like snowflakes in flight!
They coax and pull their young ones down from
the branches
to drink and frolic with the water-borne moon.

Li Po, A.D. 705–762

THE FALLOW DEER AT THE LONELY HOUSE

One without looks in tonight
Through the curtain-chink
From the sheet of glistening white;
One without looks in tonight
As we sit and think
By the fender-brink.

We do not discern those eyes
Watching in the snow;
Lit by lamps of rosy dyes
We do not discern those eyes
Wondering, aglow,
Fourfooted, tiptoe.

Thomas Hardy, 1840–1928

The fender is a low rail that goes around a fireplace.

THE TYGER

Tyger! Tyger! burning bright
In the forests of the night,
What immortal hand or eye
Could frame thy fearful symmetry?

In what distant deeps or skies
Burnt the fire of thine eyes?
On what wings dare he aspire?
What the hand dare sieze the fire?

And what shoulder, & what art,
Could twist the sinews of thy heart?
And when thy heart began to beat,
What dread hand? & what dread feet?

What the hammer? what the chain?
In what furnace was thy brain?
What the anvil? what dread grasp
Dare its deadly terrors clasp?

When the stars threw down their
spears
And water'd heaven with their tears,
Did he smile his work to see?
Did he who made the Lamb make
thee?

Tyger! Tyger! burning bright
In the forests of the night,
What immortal hand or eye
Dare frame thy fearful symmetry?

William Blake, 1757–1827

What would it be like to see a powerful tiger being constructed by miraculous machinery in a supernatural factory? (William Blake is the artist here as well as the poet.)

78

79

POEM

As the cat
climbed over
the top of

the jamcloset
first the right
forefoot

carefully
then the hind
stepped down

into the pit of
the empty
flowerpot

William Carlos
Williams
1883–1963

From JUBILATE AGNO

For I will consider my Cat Jeoffry.

. . . .

For having done duty and received blessing he begins to consider himself.
For this he performs in ten degrees.

For first he looks upon his forepaws to see if they are clean.
For secondly he kicks up behind to clear away there.
For thirdly he works it upon stretch with the forepaws extended.
For fourthly he sharpens his paws by wood.
For fifthly he washes himself.
For sixthly he rolls upon wash.
For seventhly he fleas himself, that he may not be interrupted upon the beat.
For eighthly he rubs himself against a post.
For ninthly he looks up for his instructions.
For tenthly he goes in quest of food.

80

For having considered God and himself he will consider his neighbor.
For if he meets another cat he will kiss her in kindness.
For when he takes his prey he plays with it to give it a chance.
For one mouse in seven escapes by his dallying.
For when his day's work is done his business more properly begins.
For he keeps the Lord's watch in the night against the adversary.
For he counteracts the powers of darkness by his electrical skin and glaring eyes.
For he counteracts the Devil, who is death, by brisking about the life.
For in his morning orisons he loves the sun and the sun loves him.
For he is of the tribe of Tiger.

. . . .

Christopher Smart, 1722–1771

THE OWL

The owl hooted and told of
    the morning star,
He hooted again and told of
    the dawn.

        Hopi Indians, North America

WILD GOOSE, WILD GOOSE

Wild goose, wild goose,
At what age
Did you make your first journey?

        Issa, 1763–1823?

81

82

80 Details of *Des chats: images sans paroles*. Théophile-Alexandre Steinlen, French, 1859–1923. Linocuts. Paris, Flammarion, n.d.

81 Detail of a satin panel couched in gold and embroidered with colored silks. Chinese, 19th century

82 *Wild Geese Flying down across the Moon*. Utagawa Hiroshige, Japanese, 1797–1858. Woodblock print, about 1833

83 Detail of a hanging scroll. Chu Ling, Chinese, 19th century. Ink and colors on paper, ca. 1800

83

THE CAT AND THE MOON

The cat went here and there
And the moon spun round like a top,
And the nearest kin of the moon,
The creeping cat, looked up.
Black Minnaloushe stared at the moon,
For, wander and wail as he would,
The pure cold light in the sky
Troubled his animal blood.
Minnaloushe runs in the grass
Lifting his delicate feet.
Do you dance, Minnaloushe, do you dance?
When two close kindred meet,
What better than call a dance?
Maybe the moon may learn,
Tired of that courtly fashion,
A new dance turn.
Minnaloushe creeps through the grass
From moonlit place to place,
The sacred moon overhead
Has taken a new phase.
Does Minnaloushe know that his pupils
Will pass from change to change,
And that from round to crescent,
From crescent to round they range?
Minnaloushe creeps through the grass
Alone, important and wise,
And lifts to the changing moon
His changing eyes.

        William Butler Yeats, 1865–1939

The cat, Minnaloushe, and the moon are nightly companions, wide awake and vigilant while everyone sleeps.

MEDITATIONS OF A PARROT

Oh the rocks and the thimble
The oasis and the bed
Oh the jacket and the roses.

All sweetly stood up the sea to me
Like blue cornflakes in a white bowl.
The girl said, "Watch this."

I come from Spain, I said.
I was purchased at a fair.
She said, "None of us know.

"There was a house once
Of dazzling canopies
And halls like a keyboard.

"These the waves tore in pieces."
(His old wound—
And all day! Robin Hood! Robin Hood!)

John Ashbery, b. 1927

If you could hear the thoughts of a parrot, they might sound like this.

84

PEACOCK

Think how a peacock in a forest of high trees
shimmers in a stream of blueness and long-tressed
  magnificence!
And women even cut their shimmery hair!

D. H. Lawrence, 1885–1930

85

64

BUTTERFLY

Butterfly, the wind blows sea-ward, strong beyond the garden wall!
Butterfly, why do you settle on my shoe, and sip the dirt on my shoe,
Lifting your veined wings, lifting them? big white butterfly!

Already it is October, and the wind blows strong to the sea
from the hills where snow must have fallen, the wind is polished
    with snow.
Here in the garden, with red geraniums, it is warm, it is warm
but the wind blows strong to sea-ward, white butterfly, content on
    my shoe!

Will you go, will you go from my warm house?
Will you climb on your big soft wings, black-dotted,
as up an invisible rainbow, an arch
till the wind slides you sheer from the arch-crest
and in a strange level fluttering you go out to sea-ward, white speck!

D. H. Lawrence, 1885–1930

They look
Like newlyweds
Those two butterflies.

Ryōta, 1718–1787

It's the end of the summer and this butterfly,
like a traveler following a secret
schedule, leaves the beautiful
garden for a journey
over the sea.

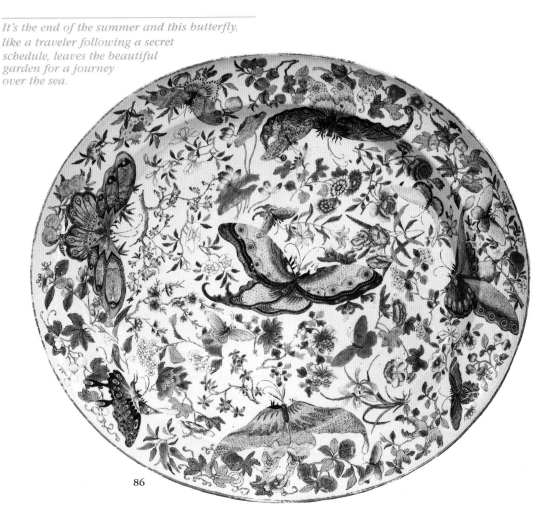

86

84 *Woman with a Parrot.* Edouard
   Manet, French, 1832–1883. Oil on
   canvas

85 Mayurī or peacock fiddle. Wood,
   feathers, and other materials.
   Northern Indian, 19th century

86 Platter with butterflies, fruits, and
   flowers. Hard-paste porcelain,
   decorated in polychrome enamel
   colors and gilt. Made in China for
   the western market, 19th century

87 Detail of a handscroll. Ma Ch'uan,
   Chinese, 1720–1800. Colors
   on paper

88, 90 Woodcuts from *Hortus sanitatis.* Strasbourg, Johann Prüss, ca. 1497

89 Detail of a color lithograph. Maria Likarz, Austrian, 1893–? Vienna, the Wiener Werkstätte

91 Woodblock print. Kitagawa Utamaro, Japanese, 1753–1806. Detail of plate 9 from *Picture Book of Selected Insects,* 1788

92 Detail of a satin panel couched in gold and embroidered with colored silks. Chinese, 19th century

93 Offering object, gold. Columbian (Muisca), 14th–16th century

94 Detail of an illustration from *Modern Poster Annual,* volume 5. New York, A. Broun, 1928

88

WHERE THE BEE SUCKS

Where the bee sucks, there suck I:
   In a cowslip's bell I lie;
There I couch when owls do cry.
On the bat's back I do fly
After summer merrily:
   Merrily, merrily, shall I live now,
   Under the blossom that hangs on
the bough.

William Shakespeare, 1564–1616

This poem is a letter from the fly, who reminds the bee to be back in time for the beginning of spring.

BEE! I'M EXPECTING YOU!

Bee! I'm expecting you!
Was saying Yesterday
To Somebody you know
That you were due—

The Frogs got Home last Week—
Are settled, and at work—
Birds, mostly back—
The Clover warm and thick—

You'll get my Letter by
The seventeenth; Reply
Or better, be with me—
Yours, Fly.

Emily Dickinson, 1830–1886

89

GRASSHOPPERS

Grasshoppers go in many a thrumming spring
And now to stalks of tasselled sour-grass cling,
That shakes and sways awhile, but still keeps
   straight,
While arching oxeye doubles with his weight.
Next on the cat-tail grass with farther bound
He springs, that bends until they touch the
   ground.

John Clare, 1793–1864

SPIDER

   With what voice,
And what song would you sing, spider,
   In this autumn breeze?

Bashō, 1644–1694

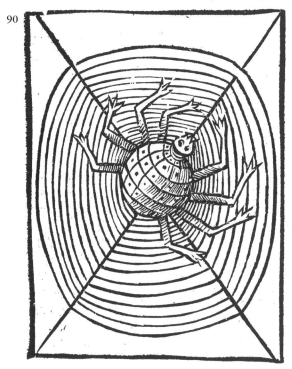

90

91

ON THE GRASSHOPPER AND CRICKET

The poetry of earth is never dead:
    When all the birds are faint with the hot sun,
    And hide in cooling trees, a voice will run
From hedge to hedge about the new-mown mead;
That is the Grasshopper's—he takes the lead
    In summer luxury,—he has never done
    With his delights; for when tired out with fun
He rests at ease beneath some pleasant weed.
The poetry of earth is ceasing never:
    On a lone winter evening, when the frost
      Has wrought a silence, from the stove there shrills
The Cricket's song, in warmth increasing ever,
    And seems to one in drowsiness half lost,
      The Grasshopper's among some grassy hills.

John Keats, 1795–1821

THREE ANIMALS

THE BUTTERFLY
The butterfly
flies up like pow
der to a woman's face
and drifts down
like a woman's face to pow
der

92

THE ELECTRIC EEL
The electric eel
slides through the water
forming different words as it goes
when it spells
"eel"
it lights up

93

THE GIRAFFE
The 2 f's
in giraffe
are like
2 giraffes
running through
the word giraffe

The 2 f's
run through giraffe
like 2 giraffes

Ron Padgett, b. 1942

94

95 Detail of a color lithograph.
Mela Koehler, Austrian, 1885–1960.
Vienna, the Wiener Werkstätte

96 Fish, bronze. Ghana, Ashanti people,
19th–20th century

97 *Mi-gyaūn* or crocodile zither.
Wood and ivory. Burmese

98 *Prince Riding on an Elephant.*
Leaf from an album attributed
to Khem Karan. Ink, colors, and gold
on paper. Mughal, Period of Akbar
(1556–1605), late 16th century

PIG

With sun on his back and sun on his belly,
His head as big and unmoving
As a cannon,
The pig is working.

Paul Eluard, 1895–1952

95

96

LITTLE FISH

The tiny fish enjoy themselves
in the sea.
Quick little splinters of life,
their little lives are fun to them
in the sea.

D. H. Lawrence, 1885–1930

HOW DOTH THE LITTLE CROCODILE

How doth the little crocodile
Improve his shining tail,
And pour the waters of the Nile
On every golden scale!

How cheerfully he seems to grin,
How neatly spreads his claws,
And welcomes little fishes in
With gently smiling jaws!

Lewis Carroll, 1832–1898

97

From ELEPHANT

Gross innocent,
Saint Elephant,
blessed beast
of the perduring forests,
bulk of our palpable world
in its counterpoise,
mighty
and exquisite,
a saddlery's cosmos
in leather,
ivory
packed into satins
unmoved
like
the flesh of the moon,
minimal eyes
to observe, without being
   observed,
horn
virtuoso
and bugling
propinquity,
animal
waterspout
elate
in
its
cleanliness,
portable
engine
and telephone booth in
   a forest:
so
softly you go
in your swagger. . . .
. . . .

   Pablo Neruda, 1904–1973

98

THE ELEPHANT

Elephant, who brings death.
Elephant, a spirit in the bush.
With a single hand
He can pull two palm trees to the ground.
If he had two hands
He would tear the sky like an old rag.
The spirit who eats dog,

The spirit who eats ram,
The spirit who eats
A whole palm fruit with its thorns.
With his four mortal legs
He tramples down the grass.
Wherever he walks
The grass is forbidden to stand up again.

   Yoruba people, Africa

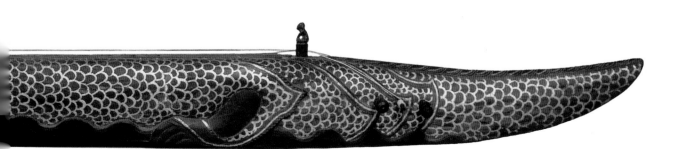

THE WORLD'S WANDERERS

Poets and artists have often felt a dramatic connection between their own feelings and the world, the whole universe, around them.

Tell me, thou Star, whose wings of light
Speed thee in thy fiery flight,
In what cavern of the night
    Will thy pinions close now?

Tell me, Moon, thou pale and gray
Pilgrim of Heaven's homeless way,
In what depth of night or day
    Seekest thou repose now?

Weary Wind, who wanderest
Like the world's rejected guest,
Hast thou still some secret nest
    On the tree or billow?

Percy Bysshe Shelley, 1792–1822

99

煙開蘭葉香風暖
岸夾桃花錦浪生
李青蓮灩澦洲的清湘老
人濟時宗招出引興

99 Detail of a set design for the entrance of the Queen of the Night in *The Magic Flute.* Karl Friedrich Thiele, active 1780–1836, after Karl Friedrich Schinkel, German, 1781–1841. Hand- and plate-colored aquatint, 1819

100 *Riverbank of Peach Blossoms.* Tao-chi (Shih-T'ao), Chinese, 1642–1707. Ink and colors on paper, from an album of twelve leaves

101 *From the Summit of Mount Huang.* K'un-ts'an, Chinese, 1612–ca. 1686. Ink and light color on paper

VIEWING THE WATERFALL AT MOUNT LU

Sunlight streaming on Incense Stone kindles violet
 smoke;
far off I watch the waterfall plunge to the long river,
flying waters descending straight three thousand feet,
till I think the Milky Way has tumbled from the
 ninth height of Heaven.

Li Po, A.D. 705–762

100

STILL NIGHT THOUGHTS

Moonlight in front of my bed—
I took it for frost on the ground!
I lift my eyes to watch the mountain moon,
lower them and dream of home.

Li Po

SPRING NIGHT IN LO-YANG—HEARING A FLUTE

In what house, the jade flute that sends these dark notes drifting,
scattering on the spring wind that fills Lo-yang?
Tonight if we should hear the willow-breaking song,
who could help but long for the gardens of home?

Li Po

THEY SAY YOU'RE STAYING IN A MOUNTAIN TEMPLE

They say you're staying in a mountain temple,
in Hang-chou—or is it Yüeh-chou?
In the wind and grime of war, how long since we parted!
At Chiang-han, bright autumns waste away.
While my shadow rests by monkey-loud trees,
my soul whirls off to where shell-born towers rise.
Next year on floods of spring I'll go downriver,
to the white clouds at the end of the east I'll look for you!

Tu Fu, A.D. 712–770

THINKING OF EAST MOUNTAIN

It's been so long since I headed for East Mountain—
how many times have the roses bloomed?
White clouds have scattered themselves away—
and this bright moon—whose house is it setting on?

Li Po

101

TO THE MOON

I remember, gracious, graceful moon
When just a year ago, upon this hill
I came, filled with pain, to gaze at you
And you were hanging then above that woods
As you are now, and brightening everything.
Your face, however, then looked dim and trembling
To me, because I saw it through the tears
Rising to my eyes, my life was so
Unhappy, and still is, and doesn't change
O my beloved moon. And yet it pleases me
This memory, and to feel again the time
Of my unhappiness. How good it is
In youthful years, when hope is still far-reaching
And memory does not go back so far
To go back to past things, even when those things
Are sad, and when the sadness has not ended!

Giacomo Leopardi, 1798–1837

TO THE MOON

Art thou pale for weariness
Of climbing heaven and gazing on the earth,
    Wandering companionless
Among the stars that have a different birth, —
And ever changing, like a joyless eye
That finds no object worth its constancy?

Percy Bysshe Shelley, 1792–1822

SO, WE'LL GO NO MORE A-ROVING

So, we'll go no more a-roving
    So late into the night,
Though the heart be still as loving,
    And the moon be still as bright.

For the sword outwears its sheath,
    And the soul wears out the breast,
And the heart must pause to breathe,
    And love itself have rest.

Though the night was made for loving,
    And the day returns too soon,
Yet we'll go no more a-roving
    By the light of the moon.

Lord Byron, 1788–1824

102 *Late Afternoon—Venice.* Edward J. Steichen, American, 1879–1973.
    Gelatin carbon photograph with selectively applied yellowtone, 1907

103 Lid of a writing box. Black lacquer. Japanese, early 19th century

104 Engraving from *Ethica naturalis, seu documenta moralia.*
    Christopher Weigel, German. Nuremberg, ca. 1700

105 Stained and painted glass. Austrian, ca. 1390

106 One of a pair of candlesticks. Silver. French (Paris), 1724–25

WAITING BOTH

A star looks down at me,
And says: "Here I and you
Stand each in our degree:
What do you mean to do,—
    Mean to do?"

I say: "For all I know,
Wait, and let Time go by,
Till my change come." — "Just so,"
The star says: "So mean I:—
    So mean I."

Thomas Hardy, 1840–1928

104

105

THE MOON RISES

When the moon comes up
the bells are lost
and there appear
impenetrable paths.

When the moon comes up
the sea blankets the earth
and the heart feels
like an island in infinity.

No one eats oranges
under the full moon.
One must eat
cold green fruit.

When the moon comes up
with a hundred equal faces,
silver money
sobs in the pocket.

Federico García Lorca
1899–1936

SILVER

Slowly, silently, now the moon
Walks the night in her silver shoon;
This way, and that, she peers, and sees
Silver fruit upon silver trees;
One by one the casements catch
Her beams beneath the silvery thatch;
Couched in his kennel, like a log,
With paws of silver sleeps the dog;
From their shadowy cote the white
    breasts peep
Of doves in a silver-feathered sleep;
A harvest mouse goes scampering by,
With silver claws and silver eye;
And moveless fish in the water gleam,
By silver reeds in a silver stream.

Walter de la Mare, 1873–1956

106

*As the moon rises, it's as if the lights go up in an imaginary
theater and an imaginary drama begins.*

107 *Allegory of the Planets
and Continents.*
Giovanni Battista Tiepolo,
Italian (Venetian),
1696–1770. Oil on canvas

108 *Autumn River.*
Wolf Kahn, American,
b. 1927. Oil on canvas

107

HEAVEN

O who will show me those delights on high?
      Echo.   I.
Thou Echo, thou art mortal, all men know.
      Echo.   No.
Wert thou not born among the trees and leaves?
      Echo.   Leaves.
And are there any leaves, that still abide?
      Echo.   Bide.
What leaves are they? impart the matter wholly.
      Echo.   Holy.

Are holy leaves the Echo then of bliss?
      Echo.   Yes.
Then tell me, what is that supreme delight?
      Echo.   Light.
Light to the mind: what shall the will enjoy?
      Echo.   Joy.
But are there cares and business with the pleasure?
      Echo.   Leisure.
Light, joy, and leisure; but shall they persevere?
      Echo.   Ever.

George Herbert, 1593–1633

I WANDERED LONELY AS A CLOUD

I wandered lonely as a cloud
That floats on high o'er vales and hills,
When all at once I saw a crowd,
A host, of golden daffodils;
Beside the lake, beneath the trees,
Fluttering and dancing in the breeze.

Continuous as the stars that shine
And twinkle on the milky way,
They stretched in never-ending line
Along the margin of a bay:
Ten thousand saw I at a glance,
Tossing their heads in sprightly dance.

The waves beside them danced; but
  they
Out-did the sparkling waves in glee:
A poet could not but be gay,
In such a jocund company:
I gazed—and gazed—but little thought
What wealth the show to me had
  brought:

For oft, when on my couch I lie
In vacant or in pensive mood,
They flash upon that inward eye
Which is the bliss of solitude;
And then my heart with pleasure fills,
And dances with the daffodils.

William Wordsworth, 1770–1850

108

*In this poem, Nature
is a peaceful queen
who only ventures out
when her ferocious
enemy, the wind, has
gone away.*

THE WIND TOOK UP
THE NORTHERN THINGS

The Wind took up the Northern Things
And piled them in the south—
Then gave the East unto the West
And opening his mouth

The four Divisions of the Earth
Did make as to devour
While everything to corners slunk
Behind the awful power—

The Wind—unto his Chambers went
And nature ventured out—
Her subjects scattered into place
Her systems ranged about

Again the smoke from Dwellings rose
The Day abroad was heard—
How intimate, a Tempest past
The Transport of the Bird—

Emily Dickinson, 1830–1886

From TO A SKYLARK

Up with me! up with me into the clouds!
    For thy song, Lark, is strong;
Up with me, up with me into the clouds!
    Singing, singing,
With clouds and sky about thee ringing. . . .

. . . .

William Wordsworth

109

STOPPING BY WOODS
ON A SNOWY EVENING

Whose woods these are I think I know,
His house is in the village though;
He will not see me stopping here
To watch his woods fill up with snow.

My little horse must think it queer,
To stop without a farmhouse near
Between the woods and frozen lake
The darkest evening of the year.

He gives his harness bells a shake
To ask if there is some mistake,
The only other sound's the sweep
Of easy wind and downy flake.

The woods are lovely dark and deep;
But I have promises to keep
And miles to go before I sleep:
And miles to go before I sleep.

Robert Frost, 1874–1963

SENSATION

On blue summer evenings I'll go
  down the pathways
Pricked by the grain, crushing the
  tender grass—
Dreaming, I'll feel its coolness on my
  feet.
I'll let the wind bathe my bare head.

I won't talk at all, I won't think about
  anything.
But infinite love will rise in my soul,
And I'll go far, very far, like a gypsy,
Into Nature—happy, as if with a
  woman.

Arthur Rimbaud, 1854–1891

110

76

THE WAKING

I strolled across
An open field;
The sun was out;
Heat was happy.

This way! This way!
The wren's throat
    shimmered,
Either to other,
The blossoms sang.

The stones sang,
The little ones did,
And flowers jumped
Like small goats.

A ragged fringe
Of daisies waved;
I wasn't alone
In a grove of apples.

Far in the wood
A nestling sighed;
The dew loosened
Its morning smells.

I came where the river
Ran over stones:
My ears knew
An early joy.

And all the waters
Of all the streams
Sang in my veins
That summer day.

Theodore Roethke
1908–1963

AFTERNOON ON A HILL

I will be the gladdest thing
    Under the sun!
I will touch a hundred flowers
    And not pick one.

I will look at cliffs and clouds
    With quiet eyes,
Watch the wind bow down
    the grass,
    And the grass rise.

And when lights begin to
    show
    Up from the town,
I will mark which must be
    mine,
    And then start down!

Edna St. Vincent Millay, 1892–1950

109 *Path in the Ile Saint-Martin,
Vétheuil* (detail). Claude Monet,
French, 1840–1926. Oil on canvas,
1880

110 *Snow Flurries*. John Fabian
Carlson, American, 1875–1945.
Oil on canvas

111 *Apple Trees in Bloom*. Claude
Monet, French, 1840–1926. Oil on
canvas, 1873

FOR THE MOMENT

Life is simple and gay
The bright sun rings with a quiet sound
The sound of the bells has quieted down
This morning the light hits it all
The footlights of my head are lit again
And the room I live in is finally bright

Just one beam is enough
Just one burst of laughter
My joy that shakes the house
Restrains those wanting to die
By the notes of its song

I sing off-key
Ah it's funny
My mouth open to every breeze
Spews mad notes everywhere
That emerge I don't know how
To fly toward other ears

Listen I'm not crazy
I laugh at the bottom of the stairs
Before the wide-open door
In the sunlight scattered
On the wall among green vines
And my arms are held out toward you

It's today I love you

Pierre Reverdy, 1889–1960

112

"I've just come up
From a place on the bottom" is the look
On the little duck's face.

Jōsō, 1662–1704

Beside the road
Mallow flowers bloom—
Now eaten by my horse!

Bashō

Well, let's go
Up to the place
Where we'll fall down and look at the snow!

Bashō, 1644–1694

First cold rain—
Even the monkey seems to want
A little straw coat.

Bashō

How cool it feels
To take a noonday nap
With my feet against a wall!

Bashō

113

The haiku is a Japanese poem that has 17 syllables. In a haiku it is as if a beautiful, brief moment is being seen in slow motion.

On the temple bell
Settles—and is sleeping—
A butterfly.

Buson, 1716–1784

112 *The Terrace at Vernon* (detail). Pierre Bonnard, French, 1867–1947. Oil on canvas, ca. 1920–39

113 Line illustrations from the *Manga,* a series of sketchbooks. Katsushika Hokusai, Japanese, 1760–1849

No one spoke,
The host, the guest
The white chrysanthemums.

Ryōta, 1718–1787

May rains!
Now frogs are swimming
At my door.

Sanpū, 1647–1732

One person
And one fly
In the big waiting room.

Issa, 1763–1823?

From SONG OF MYSELF

The pure contralto sings in the organloft,
The carpenter dresses his plank . . . . the tongue of his foreplane
    whistles its wild ascending lisp,
The married and unmarried children ride home to their
    thanksgiving dinner,
The pilot seizes the king-pin, he heaves down with a strong
    arm,
The mate stands braced in the whaleboat, lance and harpoon
    are ready,
The duck-shooter walks by silent and cautious stretches,
The deacons are ordained with crossed hands at the altar,
The spinning-girl retreats and advances to the hum of the
    big wheel,
The farmer stops by the bars of a Sunday and looks at the
    oats and rye . . . .
. . . .

The bugle calls in the ballroom, the gentlemen run for their
    partners, the dancers bow to each other;
The youth lies awake in the cedar-roofed garret and harks to
    the musical rain,
The Wolverine sets traps on the creek that helps fill the
    Huron . . . .
. . . .

The deckhands make fast the steamboat, the plank is thrown
    for the shoregoing passengers,
The young sister holds out the skein, the elder sister winds
    it off in a ball and stops now and then for the knots,
The one-year wife is recovering and happy, a week ago she
    bore her first child,
The cleanhaired Yankee girl works with her sewing-machine
    or in the factory or mill,

The nine months' gone is in the parturition chamber, her
    faintness and pains are advancing;
The pavingman leans on his twohanded rammer—the
    reporter's lead flies swiftly over the notebook—the
    signpainter is lettering with red and gold,
The canal-boy trots on the towpath—the bookkeeper counts
    at his desk—the shoemaker waxes his thread,
The conductor beats time for the band and all the performers
    follow him,
The child is baptised—the convert is making the first
    professions,
The regatta is spread on the bay . . . . how the white sails
    sparkle . . . .
. . . .

Patriarchs sit at supper with sons and grandsons and great
    grandsons around them,
In walls of adobie, in canvas tents, rest hunters and trappers
    after their day's sport.
The city sleeps and the country sleeps,
The living sleep for their time . . . . the dead sleep for their time,
The old husband sleeps by his wife and the young husband
    sleeps by his wife;
And these one and all tend inward to me, and I tend outward
    to them,
And such as it is to be of these more or less I am.

Walt Whitman, 1819–1892

America, in Whitman's time, must have been inspiring—vast, new, and
undiscovered. This poem reflects that. It is vast (1,346 lines long) and
always changing, as if a poet, like an American pioneer, could be
adventurous, inventive, and free.

TO A POOR OLD WOMAN

munching a plum on
the street a paper bag
of them in her hand

They taste good to her
They taste good
to her. They taste
good to her.

You can see it by
the way she gives herself
to the one half
sucked out in her hand

Comforted
a solace of ripe plums
seeming to fill the air
They taste good to her

William Carlos Williams

115

116

THE RED WHEELBARROW

so much depends
upon

a red wheel
barrow

glazed with rain
water

beside the white
chickens

William Carlos Williams
1883–1963

*This song is like a photograph of
ordinary life on an ordinary day.*

SONG

I'm about to go shopping.
It rained in the night.
The cat is asleep on a
clothes hamper. The roses
are mouldy. Humidity.
The sun goes in and comes out.
I have a letter to answer.
A postcard won't do. This
time, God willing, I'll
remember the Ivory Snow.

James Schuyler, b. 1923

117

CUCKOO

Repeat that, repeat,
Cuckoo, bird, and open ear wells, heart-springs, delightfully
sweet,
With a ballad, with a ballad, a rebound
Off trundled timber and scoops of the hillside ground, hollow
hollow hollow ground:
The whole landscape flushes on a sudden at a sound.

Gerard Manley Hopkins, 1844–1889

118 *Exactitude.* Pierre Fix-Masseau, French, b. 1905. Gouache, after poster of 1929

119 *Early Spring* (detail). Hobson Pittman, American, 1899–1972. Oil on canvas, 1936–37

118

IN A TRAIN

There has been a light snow.
Dark car tracks move in out of the darkness.
I stare at the train window marked with soft dust.
I have awakened at Missoula, Montana, utterly happy.

Robert Bly, b. 1926

SOME GOOD THINGS TO BE SAID FOR THE IRON AGE

A ringing tire iron
  dropped on the pavement

Whang of a saw
brusht on limbs

the taste
of rust.

Gary Snyder, b. 1930

Supposedly unpoetic things—like iron or rust—can actually be good subjects for poetry.

119

THE PASTURE

I'm going out to clean the pasture spring;
I'll only stop to rake the leaves away
(And wait to watch the water clear, I may):
I sha'n't be gone long. —You come too.

I'm going out to fetch the little calf
That's standing by the mother. It's so young,
It totters when she licks it with her tongue.
I sha'n't be gone long. —*You come too.*

Robert Frost, 1874–1963

120 Color lithograph. Théophile-
Alexandre Steinlen, French,
1859–1924

121 *From My Studio Window* (detail).
John Kane, American, 1860–1934.
Oil on canvas, 1932

121

CHOCOLATE MILK

Oh God! It's great!
to have someone fix you
chocolate milk
and to appreciate their doing it!
Even as they stir it
in the kitchen
your mouth is going crazy
for the chocolate milk!
The wonderful chocolate milk!

Ron Padgett, b. 1942

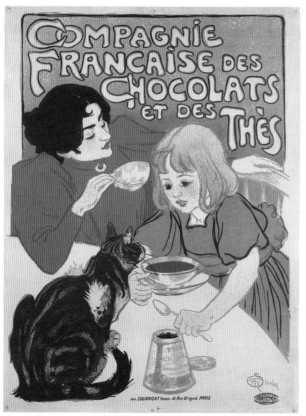
120

BALLAD OF THE MORNING STREETS

The magic of the day is the morning
I want to say the day is morning high
and sweet, good
morning.

The ballad of the morning streets, sweet
voices turns
of cool warm weather
high around the early windows grey to blue
and down again amongst the kids and
broken signs, is pure love magic, sweet day
come into me, let me live with you
and dig your blazing

Amiri Baraka, b. 1934

SONG FORM

Morning uptown, quiet on the street,
no matter the distinctions that can be
made, quiet, very quiet, on the street.
Sun's not even up, just some kid and me,
skating, both of us, at the early sun, and
amazed there is grace for us, without our
having to smile too tough, or be very pleasant
even to each other. Merely to be mere, ly to be

Amiri Baraka

122

CONVALESCENCE

To have been a little ill
To relax
To have Glucose and Bemax
    To be still.

To feel definitely weak
On a diet
To be ordered to be quiet,
    Not to speak.

To skim through the morning news,
To have leisure,
The ineffable, warm pleasure
    Of a snooze.

To have cooling things to drink,
Fresh Spring Flowers,
To have hours and hours and hours
    Just to think.

To have been a little ill
To have time
To invent a little rhyme
    To be still.

To have no one that you miss
    This is bliss!

        Noël Coward, 1899–1973

THE WIND IS BLOWING WEST

1

I am trying to decide to go swimming,
But the sea looks so calm.
All the other boys have gone in.
I can't decide what to do.

I've been waiting in my tent
Expecting to go in.
Have you forgotten to come down?
Can I escape going in?
I was just coming

I was just going in
But lost my pail

2

A boisterous tide is coming up;
I was just looking at it.
The pail is near me
again. My shoulders have sand on them.

Round the edge of the tide
Is the shore. The shore
Is filled with waves.
They are tin waves.

Boisterous tide coming up.
The tide is getting less.

3

Daytime is not a brain,
Living is not a cricket's song.
Why does light diffuse
As earth turns away from the sun?

I want to give my food
To a stranger. I want
to be taken.
What kind of a face do

I have while leaving?
I'm thinking of my friend.

4

I am trying to go swimming
But the sea looks so calm
All boys are gone
I can't decide what to do

122 *La Convalescente, Mme Lepère*. Auguste Lepère,
    French, 1849–1918. Woodcut, 1892

123 *High Tide: The Bathers*. Winslow Homer,
    American, 1836–1910. Oil on canvas, 1870

I've been waiting to go
Have you come down?
Can I escape

I am just coming
      Just going in

Joseph Ceravolo, b. 1934

This poem is about an ordinary day at the beach, but the boy's secret feelings about the day seem complicated and uncertain.

At times, life can seem as
strange as a dream.
Poets and artists have sometimes wanted to make
works as surprising and free
and obviously imaginative
as the strangest dreams,
to show something about life
that can't be described
realistically and logically.

SLEEPING ON THE CEILING

It is so peaceful on the ceiling!
It is the Place de la Concorde.
The little crystal chandelier
is off, the fountain is in the dark.
Not a soul is in the park.

Below, where the wallpaper
    is peeling,
the Jardin des Plantes has
    locked its gates.
Those photographs are animals.
The mighty flowers and
    foliage rustle;
under the leaves the insects tunnel.

We must go under the wallpaper
to meet the insect-gladiator,
to battle with a net and trident,
and leave the fountain and the
    square.
But oh, that we could sleep
    up there....

Elizabeth Bishop, 1911–1979

*Sometimes, just before going to sleep, you
may experience the odd sensation of being
in between the room where you really are
and the imaginary world of your dreams.*

WHO IS THE EAST?

Who is the East?
The Yellow Man
Who may be Purple if He can
That carries in the Sun.

Who is the West?
The Purple Man
Who may be Yellow if He can
That lets Him out again.

Emily Dickinson, 1830–1886

DAWN

I embraced the summer dawn.

Nothing was stirring yet in front of the palaces. The water lay lifeless. Encamped shadows did not leave the woodland road. I stepped forth, arousing breaths alive and warm, and precious stones kept watch, and wings rose up without a sound.

My first enterprise was, in the path already filled with cool, pale glints, a flower that told me her name.

I laughed at the blond waterfall which tossed disheveled hair across the pines: on the silvery summit I espied the goddess.

Then, one by one, I lifted her veils. In the lane, waving my arms. On the plain, where I gave the cock notice of her coming. In the city, she fled among the steeples and domes, and, running like a beggar across the marble quays, I pursued her.

On the upper part of the road, near a grove of laurels, I surrounded her with her massed veils, and I sensed somewhat her immeasurable body. Dawn and the child plunged to the bottom of the wood.

When I awoke, it was noon.

Arthur Rimbaud, 1854–1891

The boy in this poem is chasing the Dawn, who is a beautiful goddess wrapped in veils of air.

124 *Untitled.* Jerry Uelsmann, American, b. 1934. Gelatin silver photograph, 1976

125 Detail of a patchwork cover with silk embroidered panels. German, 1774

126 *Morning on the Seine near Giverny* (detail). Claude Monet, French, 1840–1926. Oil on canvas, 1897

127 *Fantastic Landscape.* Francesco Guardi, Italian (Venetian), 1712–1793. Oil on canvas

128 *Aglauros Being Changed by Mercury* (detail). One of a series of tapestries entitled *The Story of Mercury.* Woven by Willem van Pannemaker. Wool, silk, and metal thread. Flemish, 16th century

129 *Still Life: Flowers and Fruit.* Severin Roesen, American, d. ca. 1871. Oil on canvas

127

THE MOST BEAUTIFUL

1

But most beautiful of all is the Un-found Island:
The one that the King of Spain got from his cousin
The King of Portugal with the royal seal
And the papal edict written in Gothic Latin.

The Young Prince set sail for the fabulous kingdom,
He saw the Fortunate Isles: Iunonia, Gorgo, Hera
And the Sea of Sargasso and the Sea of Darkness
While looking for that island . . . But the island wasn't there.

In vain the big-bellied galleons with swollen sails,
The caravels in vain put up their rigging:
Despite the papal guarantee, the island disappeared
And Portugal and Spain are looking for her still.

2

The island exists. Appearing now and then in the distance
Between Teneriffe and Palma, veiled in mystery:
". . .the un-Found island!" The wise Canarymen
From Picco high above the Teyde point it out to the foreigner.

The pirates' ancient maps make mention of her:
"How to Find It Island," "Wandering Island"—
It is the charmed island that slips through the seas;
Sometimes the navigators see her nearby. . .

They graze with their prows that happy shore:
Amid flowers no one has ever seen the highest palm trees sway,
The heavenly forest, thick and alive, sends forth its fragrant odors,
The cardamum tree is crying, the rubber trees are oozing . . .

She is noticed first by her perfume, as a courtesan is,
The Un-found Island . . . But, if the pilot goes toward her,
Quickly she disappears, like a mirage,
Tinting herself with blue, the color of faraway.

Guido Gozzano, 1883–1916

THE SONG OF WANDERING AENGUS

This is a fairy-tale-like poem about a man who searches endlessly for a magical girl he has seen only once.

I went out to the hazel wood,
Because a fire was in my head,
And cut and peeled a hazel wand,
And hooked a berry to a thread;
And when white moths were on the wing,
And moth-like stars were flickering out,
I dropped the berry in a stream
And caught a little silver trout.

When I had laid it on the floor
I went to blow the fire aflame,
But something rustled on the floor,
And someone called me by my name:
It had become a glimmering girl
With apple blossom in her hair
Who called me by my name and ran
And faded through the brightening air.

Though I am old with wandering
Through hollow lands and hilly lands,
I will find out where she has gone,
And kiss her lips and take her hands;
And walk among long dappled grass,
And pluck till time and times are done
The silver apples of the moon,
The golden apples of the sun.

William Butler Yeats, 1865–1939

129

128

ROSE, OH PURE CONTRADICTION

Rose, oh pure contradiction, joy
of being No-one's sleep under so many
lids.

Rainer Maria Rilke, 1875–1926

These rose petals are like many eyelids softly closed over the rose's center.

DISILLUSIONMENT OF TEN O'CLOCK

The houses are haunted
By white night-gowns.
None are green,
Or purple with green rings,
Or green with yellow rings,
Or yellow with blue rings.
None of them are strange,
With socks of lace
And beaded ceintures.
People are not going
To dream of baboons and periwinkles.
Only, here and there, an old sailor,
Drunk and asleep in his boots,
Catches tigers
In red weather.

Wallace Stevens, 1879–1955

It's ten o'clock at night and the townspeople are starting to go to bed. The poet is disappointed when he thinks how boring the night clothes—and even the dreams—of the people are going to be, when they could be strange and wonderful.

132

THE GREAT FIGURE

Among the rain
and lights
I saw the figure 5
in gold
on a red
firetruck
moving
tense
unheeded
to gong clangs
siren howls
and wheels rumbling
through the dark city.

William Carlos Williams
1883–1963

Artists and poets have often inspired one another. This painting was inspired by this poem.

130

131

130 Tall clock. Maker: Jacob Diehl, American, 1776–1858. Walnut

131 *I Saw the Figure 5 in Gold*. Charles Demuth, American, 1883–1935. Oil on cardboard, 1928

132 *Stepping Out*. Roy Lichtenstein, American, b. 1923. Oil and magna on canvas

133 Dish with symmetrical floral decoration. "Damascus" ware, composite body, opaque white glaze, underglaze painted. Turkish, Iznik, mid-16th century

As Lichtenstein's painting is not a lifelike portrait of a woman, Breton's poem is not a lifelike description of his wife. Instead, it shows the happy exuberance and excitement with which he thinks of her.

From FREE UNION

My wife whose hair is a brush fire
Whose thoughts are summer lightning
Whose waist is an hourglass
Whose waist is the waist of an otter caught in the teeth of a
    tiger
Whose mouth is a bright cockade with the fragrance of a
    star of the first magnitude
Whose teeth leave prints like the tracks of white mice over
    snow
Whose tongue is made out of amber and polished glass
Whose tongue is a stabbed wafer
The tongue of a doll with eyes that open and shut
Whose tongue is incredible stone
My wife whose eyelashes are strokes in the handwriting of
    a child
Whose eyebrows are nests of swallows
My wife whose temples are the slate of greenhouse roofs
With steam on the windows
My wife whose shoulders are champagne
Are fountains that curl from the heads of dolphins under the
    ice
My wife whose wrists are matches
Whose fingers are raffles holding the ace of hearts
Whose fingers are fresh cut hay
My wife with the armpits of martens and beech fruit
And Midsummer Night
That are hedges of privet and nesting places for sea snails
Whose arms are of sea foam and a landlocked sea
And a fusion of wheat and a mill
Whose legs are spindles
In the delicate movements of watches and despair

. . . .

My wife with eyes full of tears
With eyes that are purple armor and a magnetized needle
With eyes of savannahs
With eyes full of water to drink in prisons
My wife with eyes that are forests forever under the ax
My wife with eyes that are the equal of water and air and
    earth and fire

André Breton, 1896–1966

BAVARIAN GENTIANS

Not every man has gentians in his house
in soft September, at slow, sad Michaelmas.

Bavarian gentians, big and dark, only dark
darkening the day-time, torch-like with the smoking blueness
    of Pluto's gloom,
ribbed and torch-like, with their blaze of darkness spread blue
down flattening into points, flattened under the sweep of
    white day
torch-flower of the blue-smoking darkness, Pluto's dark-blue
    daze,
black lamps from the halls of Dis, burning dark blue,
giving off darkness, blue darkness, as Demeter's pale lamps
    give off light,
lead me then, lead the way.

Reach me a gentian, give me a torch!
let me guide myself with the blue, forked touch of this
    flower
down the darker and darker stairs, where blue is darkened
    on blueness
even where Persephone goes, just now, from the frosted
    September
to the sightless realm where darkness is awake upon the dark
and Persephone herself is but a voice
or a darkness invisible enfolded in the deeper dark
of the arms Plutonic, and pierced with the passion of dense
    gloom,
among the splendour of torches of darkness, shedding
    darkness on the lost bride and her groom.

D. H. Lawrence
1885–1930

A Bavarian gentian is a deep-blue flower. In this poem, at the center of the deep blueness of the flowers there is another universe.

133

134

From LIBERTY

On my school notebooks
On my desk and the trees
On the sand on the snow
I write your name

On all the pages that have
  been read
On all the pages that are
  blank
Blood paper stone or ash
I write your name

. . . .

On every breath of dawn
On the sea on the boats
On the demented mountain
I write your name

On the foam of clouds
On the sweat of the storm
On the thick tasteless rain
I write your name

On the sparkling forms
On the bells of the colors
On the truth of bodies
I write your name

On the wakened paths
On the unfurled roads
On the overflowing market-
  places
I write your name

On the lamp being lit
On the lamp going out
On my houses all together
I write your name

On the fruit cut in two
My mirror and my bedroom
On my bed empty shell
I write your name

On my dog greedy and tender
On his trained ears
On his clumsy paw
I write your name

. . . .

On my demolished refuges
On my crumbled lighthouses
On the walls of my boredom
I write your name

On the absence without desire
On the naked solitude
On the footsteps of death
I write your name

On health that has returned
On the risk that has vanished
On hope without memory
I write your name

And through the power of a
    word
I start my life over
I am born to know who you
    are
To give you your name

Liberty

Paul Eluard, 1895–1952

---

*Eluard's passion for freedom
makes him want to write the word
Liberty all over the world.*

134 *Avenue of the Allies, Great Britain,
    1918* (detail). Childe Hassam, American,
    1859–1935. Oil on canvas, 1918

135 Woodblock print. Kitagawa Utamaro,
    Japanese, 1753–1806. Detail of plate 5
    from *Picture Book of Selected Insects,*
    1788

かきおくるみもとろと
つるこひのつけばあらむ
千枝竟元
地

135

MR. LIZARD IS CRYING
for Mademoiselle Teresita Guillén playing on a seven-note piano

Mr. lizard is crying.
Mrs. lizard is crying.

Mr. and Mrs. lizard
with little white bibs.

They have carelessly
lost their wedding ring.

Oh, their little ring of lead,
oh, their little leaden ring!

A big sky with nobody in it
rides the birds on its balloon.

The sun, that rounded captain,
wears a vest of satin.

See how old they are!
How old the lizards are!

Oh, how they cry and cry,
oh, oh, how they are crying!

Federico García Lorca, 1899–1936

These lizards are like sad, eerie animals in a scene from a disturbing dream.

136 *The Giant.* Francisco de Goya y Lucientes, Spanish, 1746–1828. Aquatint, first state

137 *The Flatiron.* Edward J. Steichen, American, 1879–1973. 1909 print from 1904 negative, blue-green pigment gum-bichromate over platinum

138 *The Lighthouse at Two Lights.* Edward Hopper, American, 1882–1967. Oil on canvas, 1929

FOG

The fog comes
on little cat feet.

It sits looking
over harbor and city
on silent haunches
and then moves on.

Carl Sandburg
1878–1967

136

137

NARCOLEPSY

The sun   like a sleepy giant
has taken an axe in his hand
    and gone into the woods
and all day long there is sound in the woods
and at dusk he has come out of the woods
and his arms are burning logs & timbers
and he laughs at the dark
and all night   it is quiet   in the woods.

Maureen Owen, b. 1942

The sun, in this poem, wakes up sleepy but works all day anyway, finishing his work, happily ablaze, at sunset. Narcolepsy is a disease in which a person can hardly stay awake.

138

CANTICLE

1

I was on a white coast once.
My father was with me on his head.
I said:
Father, father, I can't fall down.
I was born for the sun and the moon.

I looked at the clouds
and all the clouds were mounting.
My friends made a blue ring.
O we hung down with the birds.

2

I loved the snow
when the summer ran away.
Once I said:

Cricket, cricket, aren't you afraid
that you're really too loud?
He said:

David,
I don't think so.

3

Monstrous night!

I want light now! now!
I want those great stars again!
I want to know
why I keep asking my father
what he's doing on that shore.
What is he doing, anyway?
Why isn't he over here?

I saw the Red Bird too.
But where's its Wing?

I want to tell my father what I saw:
That Bird is full of fear.

David Shapiro, b. 1947

In this poem, written when David Shapiro was 14 years old, contradictory feelings of confusion, loneliness, and excitement are expressed in a dreamlike way.

As painters sometimes invent new ways to use paint, poets invent new ways to use words, to say something that can't be said with the old ways of writing poetry. Especially in our time, a painting can seem a whole new way of seeing, a poem a whole new way of speaking.

139

From TENDER BUTTONS

AN UMBRELLA

Coloring high means that the strange reason is in front not more in front behind. Not more in front in peace of the dot.

A PETTICOAT

A light white, a disgrace, an ink spot, a rosy charm.

A NEW CUP AND SAUCER

Enthusiastically hurting a clouded yellow bud and saucer, enthusiastically so is the bite in the ribbon.

RED ROSES

A cool red rose and a pink cut pink, a collapse and a sold hole, a little less hot.

COLORED HATS

Colored hats are necessary to show that curls are worn by an addition of blank spaces, this makes the difference between single lines and broad stomachs, the least thing is lightening, the least thing means a little flower and a big delay a big delay that makes more nurses than little women really little women. So clean is a light that nearly all of it shows pearls and little ways. A large hat is tall and me and all custard whole.

A SOUND

Elephant beaten with candy and little pops and chews all bolts and reckless reckless rats, this is this.

A DOG

A little monkey goes like a donkey that means to say that means to say that more sighs last goes. Leave with it. A little monkey goes like a donkey.

Gertrude Stein, 1874–1946

In her book Picasso, Gertrude Stein says that Picasso didn't paint from models because he didn't want to paint things as everyone else saw them but as he saw them. Gertrude Stein didn't want to use the language that the rest of the world used but a language that would express her own real sense of things. This language is, perhaps, more like the language of thoughts before they are organized into logical sentences.

139 *Still Life by Lamplight.* Pablo Picasso, Spanish, 1881–1973. Linoleum print, 1962

HEART CROWN AND MIRROR

```
        N  F
      W      L
      O       A   M  Y   H
      D        M E        E
      E                    A
      D                    R
      I                T
      S              L
        P          I
        U        K
          N    E
            A
```

```
              W
    T     K     H     H     D
    HE  INGS    O   AVE   IED
    ONE         BY        ONE
    ARE REBORN IN POETS' HEARTS
```

```
              IN
         IONS      THIS
       FLECT          MIR
       RE              ROR
       THE              I
       LIKE            AM
   NOT     Guillaume     EN
           Apollinaire
   AND               CLOSED
   GELS                 A
   AN                  LIVE
     GINE             AND
      MA            REAL
       I           AS
             YOU
```

Guillaume Apollinaire
1880-1918

VOWELS

Black A, white E, red I, green U, blue O—vowels,

I'll tell, some day, your secret origins:

A, black hairy corset of dazzling flies

Who boom around cruel stenches,

Gulfs of darkness; E, candor of steam and of tents,

Lances of proud glaciers, white kings, Queen-Anne's-lace shivers;

I, deep reds, spit blood, laughter of beautiful lips

In anger or in drunkenness and penitence;

U, cycles, divine vibrations of dark green oceans,

Peacefulness of pastures dotted with animals, the peace of wrinkles

Which alchemy prints on studious foreheads;

O, supreme trumpet, full of strange harsh sounds,

Silences which are crossed by Worlds and by Angels—

O, Omega, violet ray of Her Eyes!

Arthur Rimbaud, 1854–1891

This is a poem about the mysterious connections between sounds and colors, a magical vision of where the vowels come from. (The V in the illustration actually represents a U, as was common in old alphabets.)

140 Engraved letters from *The Penman's Magazine* by George Shelley. London, Thomas Read, 1705

141 *Poplars.* Claude Monet, French, 1840–1926. Oil on canvas

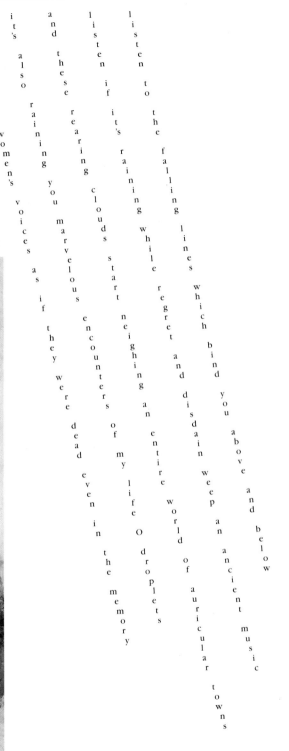

IT'S RAINING

It's raining women's voices as if they were dead even in the memory

it's also raining you marvelous encounters of my life O droplets

and these rearing clouds start neighing an entire world of auricular towns

listen if it's raining while regret and disdain weep an ancient music

listen to the falling lines which bind you above and below

Guillaume Apollinaire

The shape of a poem, like the shapes in a painting, can influence what that poem makes us feel. The shape of this poem, a rain shower of words, adds to the feeling of loneliness, longing, and loss expressed by the words.

141

PLOUGHING ON SUNDAY

The white cock's tail
Tosses in the wind.
The turkey-cock's tail
Glitters in the sun.

Water in the fields.
The wind pours down.
The feathers flare
And bluster in the wind.

Remus, blow your horn!
I'm ploughing on Sunday,
Ploughing North America.
Blow your horn!

Tum-ti-tum,
Ti-tum-tum-tum!
The turkey-cock's tail
Spreads to the sun.

The white cock's tail
Streams to the moon.
Water in the fields.
The wind pours down.

Wallace Stevens, 1879–1955

142 *Cypresses.* Vincent van Gogh,
Dutch, 1853–1890. Oil on canvas

143 *Bordighera.* Claude Monet, French,
1840–1926. Oil on canvas, 1884

142

143

PIED BEAUTY

Glory be to God for dappled things—
    For skies of couple-colour as a brinded cow;
      For rose-moles all in stipple upon trout that swim;
Fresh-firecoal chestnut-falls; finches' wings;
    Landscape plotted and pieced—fold, fallow, and plough;
      And all trades, their gear and tackle and trim.
All things counter, original, spare, strange;
    Whatever is fickle, freckled (who knows how?)
      With swift, slow; sweet, sour; adazzle, dim;
He fathers-forth whose beauty is past change:
               Praise him.

                   Gerard Manley Hopkins, 1844–1889

Try reading this poem aloud. The rough rhythms give a feeling of the exciting energy and constant movement of nature—a kind of energy and movement that is suggested, perhaps, by the brush strokes in van Gogh's painting.

up into the silence the green

up into the silence the green
silence with a white earth in it

you will (kiss me) go

out into the morning the young
morning with a warm world in it

(kiss me) you will go

on into the sunlight the fine
sunlight with a firm day in it

you will go (kiss me

down into your memory and
a memory and memory

i) kiss me (will go)

                e. e. cummings, 1894–1962

SPORTING GOODS

Brave as a postage stamp
he went his way
gently clapping his hands
to count his steps
his heart red like a wild boar
beat and beat
like a pink and green butterfly
From time to time
he planted a small satin flag
When he had marched for a long time
he sat down to rest
and fell asleep
But from that day on there've been many clouds in the sky
many birds in the trees
much salt in the sea
And also many other things

Philippe Soupault, b. 1897

Sometimes a poem or painting, like a musical composition, goes together in a way that is pleasing, without being about anything that you recognize from real life.

145

THE THINNEST SHADOW

He is sherrier
And sherriest.
A tall thermometer
Reflects him best.

Children in the street
Watch him go by.
"Is that the thinnest shadow?"
They to one another cry.

A face looks from the mirror
As if to say,
"Be supple, young man,
Since you can't be gay."

All his friends have gone
From the street corner cold.
His heart is full of lies
And his eyes are full of mold.

John Ashbery, b. 1927

144

POEM

O sole mio, hot diggety, nix "I wather think I can"
come to see *Go into Your Dance* on TV—*HELEN MORGAN!? GLENDA FARRELL!?*
1935!?
     it reminds me of my first haircut, or an elm tree or something!
or did I fall off my bicycle when my grandmother came back from Florida?

     you see I have always wanted things to be beautiful
     and now, for a change, they are!

Frank O'Hara, 1926–1966

Frank O'Hara's poems are sometimes like snapshots in which nothing seems to have been posed or artificially arranged. (The book in these photographs is a book of poetry by Frank O'Hara.)

144 *Alpha-Phi.* Morris Louis, American, 1912–1962. Acrylic on canvas, 1960

145 Relief with allegorical figures, mounted as a mirror frame. Wenzel Jamnitzer, German, 1508–1585. Silver gilt

146 *Sight/Sound: for Mike Goldberg, Samos, Greece.* Eve Sonneman, American, b. 1946. Cibachrome photograph, 1977

A TRUE ACCOUNT OF TALKING TO THE SUN AT FIRE ISLAND

The Sun woke me this morning loud
and clear, saying "Hey! I've been
trying to wake you up for fifteen
minutes. Don't be so rude, you are
only the second poet I've ever chosen
to speak to personally
                              so why
aren't you more attentive? If I could
burn you through the window I would
to wake you up. I can't hang around
here all day."
                    "Sorry, Sun, I stayed
up late last night talking to Hal."

"When I woke up Mayakovsky he was
a lot more prompt" the Sun said
petulantly. "Most people are up
already waiting to see if I'm going
to put in an appearance."
                                    I tried
to apologize "I missed you yesterday."
"That's better" he said. "I didn't
know you'd come out." "You may be
wondering why I've come so close?"
"Yes" I said beginning to feel hot
and wondering if maybe he wasn't burning me
anyway.
              "Frankly I wanted to tell you
I like your poetry. I see a lot
on my rounds and you're okay. You may
not be the greatest thing on earth, but
you're different. Now, I've heard some
say you're crazy, they being excessively
calm themselves to my mind, and other
crazy poets think that you're a boring
reactionary. Not me.
                            Just keep on
like I do and pay no attention. You'll
find that people always will complain
about the atmosphere, either too hot
or too cold too bright or too dark, days
too short or too long.
                              If you don't appear
at all one day they think you're lazy
or dead. Just keep right on, I like it.

And don't worry about your lineage
poetic or natural. The Sun shines on
the jungle, you know, on the tundra
the sea, the ghetto. Wherever you were
I knew it and saw you moving. I was waiting
for you to get to work.

                              And now that you
are making your own days, so to speak,
even if no one reads you but me
you won't be depressed. Not
everyone can look up, even at me. It
hurts their eyes."
                        "Oh Sun, I'm so grateful to you!"

"Thanks and remember I'm watching. It's
easier for me to speak to you out
here. I don't have to slide down
between buildings to get your ear.
I know you love Manhattan, but
you ought to look up more often.
                                        And
always embrace things, people earth
sky stars, as I do, freely and with
the appropriate sense of space. That
is your inclination, known in the heavens
and you should follow it to hell, if
necessary, which I doubt.
                                    Maybe we'll
speak again in Africa, of which I too
am specially fond. Go back to sleep now
Frank, and I may leave a tiny poem
in that brain of yours as my farewell."

"Sun, don't go!" I was awake
at last. "No, go I must, they're calling
me."
        "Who are they?"
                              Rising he said "Some
day you'll know. They're calling to you
too." Darkly he rose, and then I slept.

Frank O'Hara, 1926–1966

147 *The Repast of the Lion* (detail). Henri Rousseau, French,
      1844–1910. Oil on canvas

APPENDIX

ABOUT HELPING YOUNG PEOPLE TO LIKE POETRY

In describing the relation between the various art forms, the conductor Leopold Stokowski said that the need to create art was like the root system of a great oak tree, and that the different art forms—painting, poetry, music, dance, architecture—were like the different branches of the tree. It is one way to explain that the same kinds of artistic impulses lead to many different kinds of artistic expression and that all of the art forms seem to have a deep and natural imaginative connection. Because of this natural connection between the arts, great works of visual art are exciting illustrations for a collection of poetry.

We chose poems and works of art that we thought would appeal to young people, but we didn't choose works that were intended specifically for them. Those kinds of works are rarely examples of great poetry and art and it is only good poetry and art that move and excite people and inspire them to want to know more. Some of the poems in the book are harder, some are easier. We wanted this to be a book that could be read by readers of different ages, a book that a child could grow up with.

When I was a child, I loved reading poetry, even when I couldn't explain anything about it. It seemed that there were so many things that one felt and sensed that no one ever talked about or explained, things that were, perhaps, inexpressible. Poetry seemed to me to be a miraculous language in which people could, almost magically, express the exact truth about these things. Reading poetry was soothing and exciting at the same time, and satisfied an inner restlessness in a way that nothing else did. Later I found the same kind of pleasure in listening to music, in looking at paintings, or in watching a dance or a play.

Since young people's imaginative capacities are stronger and more available to them than their intellectual capacities, it's natural for them to understand poetry imaginatively even when they can't explain why intellectually. As they get older, they often become interested in thinking and talking and writing analytically about their understanding of poetry, but that process is different from understanding poetry. A reader can appreciate and get something from poetry without being good at explaining it, just as someone can be moved by the sunlight changing colors on the ocean without knowing what makes that beautiful, or can enjoy plunging into cool water for a swim without knowing what physical principles are involved in swimming. (Would children ever learn to swim if they first had to be able to explain the physics of swimming?)

When someone enjoys a wonderful painting, a beautiful building, or a good poem, he has begun to understand it. If he doesn't enjoy it, he might never understand it. With poetry, as with the other arts, pleasure leads to—and is a part of—understanding. The best way to help young people to get something from poetry is to encourage them to like whatever they seem naturally to like, perhaps also expressing one's own enjoyment, thoughts, and enthusiasm.

Since part of what makes sense of poetry is its sound, its "music," it's worth reading poems aloud. A younger child who has difficulty reading a poem is likely to enjoy it when it is read aloud. (Once, when I was reading Gertrude Stein's work aloud to some little children, their spontaneous response was to dance to it.)

The poet Wallace Stevens wrote that the function of the poet is to let "his imagination become the light in the minds of others," that the purpose of poetry is "to help us live our lives." That can be said of the other arts as well. The arts come from an inner necessity as natural and mysterious as the inner necessity that makes the oak tree grow and develop and take its shape. What poets and artists do lives after them and adds something to the world, becoming a sort of man-made natural resource, a permanent public repository of private visions of the many different ways human life has been and is and might be.

The arts perpetuate, as nothing else does, the ideal of the happiness, sanity, and harmony of life in a world that is always changing. They develop and enlighten the mind while they entertain, teach, and challenge; they enhance, inspire, suggest new possibilities, give solace, hope, and satisfaction; they add to what we know and are and can become. When you encourage young people to enjoy the arts you are helping them, perhaps, to live better lives.

Kate Farrell

ACKNOWLEDGMENTS

Grateful acknowledgement is made to the following for permission to print the copyrighted material listed below.

David Antin: "Free Union" by André Breton, translated by David Antin. Reprinted by permission of the translator.

Atheneum Publishers: W.S. Merwin, excerpted from "Liberty" in *Selected Translations 1948–1968.* Copyright © 1968 W.S. Merwin. Reprinted with the permission of Atheneum Publishers, Inc., W.S. Merwin, and Harold Ober Associates.

Blue Wind Press: "Kirsten" excerpted from *So Going Around Cities: New & Selected Poems 1958–1979,* © copyright 1980, 1985 by Ted Berrigan, reprinted here by permission of Blue Wind Press, P.O. Box 7175, Berkeley, CA 94707.

Robert Bly: "In a Train" reprinted from *Silence in the Snowy Fields.* Wesleyan University Press, 1962. Copyright © 1960 by Robert Bly. Reprinted with his permission.

Georges Borchardt, Inc.: "Meditations of a Parrot" and "The Thinnest Shadow" reprinted by permission of Georges Borchardt, Inc., and the author. Copyright © 1956 by John Ashbery.

Reed Bye: "Spring" by Reed Bye, which appeared in his collection *Some Magic at the Dump* in 1978, is reprinted by permission of the publisher, Angel Hair Books.

Cambridge University Press: "Hymn to the Sun" by Fang, "Lullaby" by Akan, "The Magnificent Bull" by Dinka, "Song for the Sun That Disappeared behind the Rainclouds" by Hottentot, and "Five Ghost Songs" by Ambo people from *African Poetry* edited by Ulli Beier reprinted by permission of the editor and Cambridge University Press.

Jonathan Cape Ltd.: "Stopping by Woods on a Snowy Evening" and "The Pasture" from *The Poetry of Robert Frost,* edited by Edward Connery Lathem, reprinted by permission of the Estate of Robert Frost, the editor, and Jonathan Cape Ltd.

Joseph Ceravolo: "The Wind Is Blowing West" reprinted by permission of the author.

Thomas Colchie Associates: Federico García Lorca, "Cancion tonta," "El lagarto esta llorando," and "La luna asoma," from *Obras Completas.* Copyright © Herederos de Federico García Lorca. All rights reserved. Permission to reprint in English translations from Thomas Colchie Associates, Inc., agents for the Estate of Federico García Lorca and, for "El lagarto esta llorando" and "La luna asoma," from the translator, William Bryant Logan.

Columbia University Press: "Autumn Cove," "Spring Night in Lo-yang—Hearing a Flute," "Still Night Thoughts," "They Say You're Staying in a Mountain Temple," "Thinking of East Mountain," and "Viewing the Waterfall at Mount Lu" from *Chinese Lyricism,* © 1971, Columbia University Press. By permission.

Doubleday & Company, Inc.: "The Waking," copyright 1948 by Theodore Roethke from the book *The Collected Poems of Theodore Roethke* by Theodore Roethke. Reprinted by permission of Doubleday & Company, Inc.

Faber and Faber Publishers: "The River Merchant's Wife" by Rihaku (Li Po) from *Collected Shorter Poems* by Ezra Pound; "The Waking" from *The Collected Poems of Theodore Roethke;* "A Rabbit as King of the Ghosts," "Disillusionment of Ten O'Clock," and "Ploughing on Sunday" from *The Collected Poems of Wallace Stevens,* reprinted by permission of Faber and Faber Ltd.

Farrar, Straus and Giroux, Inc.: "Sleeping on the Ceiling" from *Elizabeth Bishop: The Complete Poems 1927–1979.* Copyright © 1983 by Alice Helen Methfessel. Copyright © 1969 by Elizabeth Bishop. Reprinted by permission of Farrar, Straus and Giroux, Inc.

Granada Publishing Ltd.: "here's a little mouse) and" and "up into the silence the green" from *The Complete Poems 1913–1962* by e. e. cummings reprinted by permission of Granada Publishing Limited.

Maxine Groffsky Literary Agency: "I Think," "Song," and "Sunday" from *Hymn to Life,* copyright © 1972, 1973, 1974 by James Schuyler. Reprinted by permission of the author.

Grove Press: Selection from "The Elephant" from *Selected Poems of Pablo Neruda* reprinted by permission of Grove Press, Inc. Copyright © 1961 by Grove Press, Inc.

Harcourt Brace Jovanovich, Inc.: "up into the silence the green" by E. E. Cummings: Copyright 1939 by E. E. Cummings; renewed 1967 by Marion Morehouse Cummings. Reprinted from *Complete Poems 1913–1962* by E. E. Cummings by permission of Harcourt Brace Jovanovich, Inc. "Fog" by Carl Sandburg: From *Chicago Poems* by Carl Sandburg, copyright 1916 by Holt, Rinehart & Winston, Inc.; renewed 1944 by Carl Sandburg. Reprinted by permission of Harcourt Brace Jovanovich, Inc.

Harvard University Press: "Bee! I'm Expecting You!," "We Like March," "Who Is the East" and "The Wind Took up the Northern Things" reprinted by permission of the publishers and the Trustees of Amherst College from *The Poems of Emily Dickinson,* edited by Thomas H. Johnson, Cambridge, Mass.: The Belknap Press of Harvard University Press, Copyright 1951, © 1955, 1979, 1983 by The President and Fellows of Harvard College.

Holt, Rinehart & Winston: "The Pasture" and "Stopping by Woods on a Snowy Evening" from *The Poetry of Robert Frost* edited by Edward Connery Lathem. Copyright 1916, 1923, 1939, © 1967, 1969 by Holt, Rinehart and Winston. Copyright 1944, 1951 by Robert Frost. Reprinted by permission of Holt, Rinehart and Winston, Publishers. "When I Was One and Twenty" from "A Shropshire Lad"—Authorized Edition— from *The Collected Poems of A. E. Housman.* Copyright 1939, 1940, © 1965 by Robert E. Symons. Reprinted by permission of Holt, Rinehart and Winston, Publishers.

Kenneth Koch: "Sonnet" by Dante Alighieri, "To Ride" and "Pig" by Paul Eluard, "To the Moon" by Giacomo Leopardi, "Sensation" and "Vowels" by Arthur Rimbaud, and "I Want to Say Your Name" by Léopold Sédar Senghor, translated by Kenneth Koch. "Beside the road," "First cold rain," "How cool it feels," and "Well, let's go" by Bashō, "On the temple bell" by Buson, "One person" by Issa, "I've just come up" by Jōsō, "May rains!" by Sanpū, English translations by Kenneth Koch based on the word-for-word translations by Harold Henderson in *An Introduction to Haiku.*

Levin, Gann & Hankin: Selections from *Tender Buttons* by Gertrude Stein, reprinted by permission of the Estate of Gertrude Stein.

Liveright Publishing Corporation: "here's a little mouse) and" is reprinted from *IS 5 poems* by E. E. Cummings by permission of Liveright Publishing Corporation. Copyright © 1985 by E. E. Cummings. Copyright 1926 by Horace Liveright. Copyright renewed 1954 by E. E. Cummings. Copyright © 1985 by George James Firmage.

Macmillan Ltd: "The Fallow Deer at the Lonely House" and "Waiting Both" by Thomas Hardy reprinted by permission of Macmillan Ltd.

Macmillan Publishing Company: "The Song of Wandering Aengus" and "To an Isle in the Water" from *Collected Poems of W. B. Yeats* (New York: Macmillan, 1956) reprinted by permission of Macmillan Publishing Company. "The Cat and the Moon" from *The Poems of W. B. Yeats,* edited by Richard J. Finneran, copyright 1919 by Macmillan Publishing Company. Copyright renewed 1947 by Bertha Georgie Yeats.

Methuen & Company Ltd.: "Convalescence" from *Collected Verse* by Noël Coward reprinted by permission of Methuen & Company Ltd, London.

Norma Millay Ellis: "Afternoon on a Hill" and "Counting-out Rhyme" from *Collected Poems,* Harper and Row, copyright 1917, 1928, 1945, 1955 by Edna St. Vincent Millay and Norma Millay Ellis. Reprinted by permission of Norma Millay Ellis.

New Directions Publishing Corp.: "The River Merchant's Wife" by Ezra Pound from *Personae.* Copyright 1926 by Ezra Pound. Reprinted by permission of New Directions Publishing Corporation. "Wild Goose, Wild Goose" by Issa, "No One Spoke" and "Spring" by Ryōta translated by Kenneth Rexroth from *One Hundred Poems from the Japanese.* All rights reserved. "'I Am Cherry Alive' the Little Girl Sang" by Delmore Schwartz from *Selected Poems: Summer Knowledge.* Copyright © 1959 by Delmore Schwartz. Reprinted by permission of New Directions Publishing Corporation and Laurence Pollinger Limited. "Some Good Things to Be Said for the Iron Age" by Gary Snyder from *Regarding Wave.* Copyright © 1970 by Gary Snyder. Reprinted by permission of New Directions Publishing Corporation. "The Great Figure," "The Locust Tree in Flower," "Poem," "The Red Wheelbarrow," "Spring," "The Thinker," and "To a Poor Old Woman," by William Carlos Williams from *Collected Earlier Poems.* Copyright 1938 by New Directions Publishing Corporation. "Silly Song" from *The Selected Poems of Federico García Lorca,* copyright © 1955 by New Directions Publishing Corporation. Reprinted by permission of New Directions Publishing Corporation.

W. W. Norton & Company, Inc.: "From a Childhood" is reprinted from *Translations from the Poetry of Rainer Maria Rilke* by M. D. Herter Norton, by permission of W. W. Norton & Company, Inc. Copyright 1938 by W. W. Norton & Company, Inc. Copyright renewed 1966 by M. D. Herter Norton.

Harold Ober Associates: "Juke Box Love Song" by Langston Hughes from *Selected Poems,* copyright 1951 by Langston Hughes. Copyright renewed 1979 by George Houston Bass. Reprinted by permission of Harold Ober Associates.

Maureen Owen: "Narcolepsy" reprinted from *Hearts in Space,* Kulchur Press, 1980.

Oxford University Press: "Pied Beauty," and "Repeat that, repeat" by Gerard Manley Hopkins from *The Poems of Gerard Manley Hopkins* published by Oxford University Press. "Dawn" from *A Season in Hell: The Illuminations* by Arthur Rimbaud, translated by Enid Rhodes Peschel. Copyright © 1973 by Oxford University Press, Inc. Reprinted by permission.

Ron Padgett: "Chocolate Milk" by Ron Padgett from *Tulsa Kid* (Z Press) copyright 1978 by Ron Padgett. Reprinted by permission of the author. "Three Animals" and "For the Moment" reprinted by permission of the author.

Victoria Pesce: "The Most Beautiful" by Guido Gozzano, translated by Victoria Pesce. Reprinted by permission of the translator.

Penguin Books Ltd.: "Hops" reprinted from *Boris Pasternak Selected Poems* translated by Jon Stallworthy and Peter France, Penguin Books, 1984. Copyright Peter France, 1983, by permission of Penguin Books, Limited.

Laurence Pollinger, Ltd.: "Bavarian Gentians," "Butterfly," "Little Fish," "Peacock," and "The White Horse" from *The Complete Poems of D. H. Lawrence* by permission of Laurence Pollinger Limited and the Estate of Mrs. Frieda Lawrence Ravagli.

Anne Porter: "Another Sarah" printed by permission of the author.

Random House Inc, Alfred A. Knopf: "Late Last Night" from *One Way Ticket,* by Langston Hughes. Copyright 1948 by Alfred A. Knopf, Inc. Reprinted by permission of the publisher. "Miss Blues'es Child" copyright © 1959 by Langston Hughes. Reprinted from *Selected Poems of Langston Hughes,* by permission of Alfred A. Knopf, Inc. and Harold Ober Associates Incorporated. "Autobiographia Literaria" copyright © 1967 by Maureen Granville-Smith, Administratrix of the Estate of Frank O'Hara. "Poem" and "Song" copyright © 1960 by Maureen Granville-Smith, Administratrix of the Estate of Frank O'Hara. "Today" copyright © 1950 by Maureen Granville-Smith,

CREDITS

Page 57:
Purchase, Joseph Pulitzer Bequest, 1966 66.173. Charles Stewart Smith Collection, Gift of Mrs. Charles Stewart Smith, Charles Stewart Smith, Jr. and Howard Caswell Smith, in memory of Charles Stewart Smith, 1914 14.76.59 (5). Fletcher Fund, 1959 59.135.3
Page 58:
Purchase, The Dillon Fund Gift, 1977 1977.78
Page 59:
Bequest of Lizzie P. Bliss, 1931 31.67.12. Bequest of Miss Adelaide Milton de Groot (1876–1967), 1967 67.187.164. Bequest of George White Thorne, 1883 83.1.67
Page 60:
Marquand Collection, Gift of Henry G. Marquand, 1889 89.15.16. The Jack and Belle Linsky Collection, 1982 1982.60.357
Page 61:
Gift of Japan Institute, Inc., 1942, and Purchase, Seymour Fund, 1953 42.39.ab; 53.66ab. Rogers Fund, 1917 17.10.42. Gift of Otto Hufeland, 1908 08.2
Page 62:
Gift of Mrs. Edward C. Möen, 1961 61.687.12
Page 63:
Gift of Citizens' Committee for the Army, Navy and Air Force, 1962 62.218. Purchase, Joseph Pulitzer Bequest, 1918 JP 270. Rogers Fund, 1956 56.129.3
Page 64:
Gift of Erwin Davis, 1889 89.21.3. The Crosby Brown Collection of Musical Instruments, 1889 89.4.163
Page 65:
The Helena Woolworth McCann Collection, Purchase, Winfield Foundation Gift, 1970 1970.278. Fletcher Fund, 1947 47.18.116a
Page 66:
The Elisha Whittelsey Collection, The Elisha Whittelsey Fund, 1944 44.7.37. Museum Accession, 1943. The Elisha Whittelsey Collection, The Elisha Whittelsey Fund, 1944 44.7.37
Page 67:
Rogers Fund, 1918 JP1051. Gift of Citizens' Committee for the Army, Navy and Air Force, 1962 62.218. Gift of Alice K. Bache, 1974 1974.271.27; The Michael C. Rockefeller Memorial Collection, Bequest of Nelson A. Rockefeller, 1979 1979.206.740
Page 68:
Museum Accession, 1943. The Michael C. Rockefeller Memorial Collection, Gift of Nelson A. Rockefeller, 1969 1978.412.567. Gift of Miss Alice Getty, 1946 46.34.67
Page 69:
Rogers Fund, 1925 25.68.4
Page 70:
The Elisha Whittelsey Collection, The Elisha Whittelsey Fund, 1954 54.602.1(14)
Page 71:
The Sackler Fund, 1972 1972.122c. Purchase, The Dillon Fund Gift, 1973 1973.308
Page 72:
Gift of Alfred Stieglitz, 1933 33.43.50. Bequest of Stephen Whitney Phoenix, 1881 81.1.153
Page 73:
Harris Brisbane Dick Fund, by exchange, 1942 42.26.1. The Cloisters Collection, 1936 36.39.2. Bequest of Catherine D. Wentworth, 1948 48.187.392
Page 74:
Gift of Mr. and Mrs. Charles Wrightsman, 1977 1977.1.3.

Page 75:
Purchase, The Martin S. Ackerman Foundation Gift, 1979 1979.184
Page 76:
Bequest of Julia W. Emmons, 1956 56.135.1. Gift of the friends of the artist, 1947 47.46
Page 77:
Bequest of Mary Livingston Willard, 1926 26.186.1
Page 78:
Gift of Mrs. Frank Jay Gould, 1968 68.1. The Howard Mansfield Collection, Gift of Howard Mansfield, 1936
Page 80:
Gift of Mrs. Russell Sage, 1908 08.228
Page 81:
Purchase, Bequest of Charles Allen Munn, by exchange, Fosburgh Fund, Inc. and Mr. and Mrs. J. William Middendorf II Gifts, and Henry G. Keasbey Bequest, 1967 67.111. Gift of Joyce Blaffer von Bothmer, in memory of Mr. and Mrs. Robert Lee Blaffer, 1975 1975.210. Warner Communications Inc. Purchase Fund, 1976 1976.569
Page 82:
Purchase, 1983 1983.1014. George A. Hearn Fund, 1938 38.101.2
Page 83:
Bequest of Miss Adelaide Milton de Groot (1876–1967), 1967 67.187.164. Gift of Bessie Potter Vonnoh, 1941 41.12.19.
Page 84:
Purchase, Anne and Carl Stern Gift, 1970 1970.532
Pages 84-85:
Gift of Mrs. William F. Milton, 1923 23.77.3
Page 86:
Purchase, Warner Communications Inc. Gift and matching funds from the National Endowment for the Arts, 1981 1981.1073
Page 87:
Bequest of Helen Hay Whitney, 1944 45.128.7. Bequest of Julia W. Emmons, 1956 56.135.4
Page 88:
Gift of Julia A. Berwind, 1953 53.225.4
Page 89:
Bequest of George Blumenthal, 1941 41.190.134. Purchase, Bequest of Charles Allen Munn, by exchange, Fosburgh Fund, Inc. and Mr. and Mrs. J. William Middendorf II Gifts, and Henry G. Keasbey Bequest, 1967 67.111
Page 90:
Purchase, Douglas and Priscilla de Forest Williams, Mr. and Mrs. Eric M. Wunsch and The Sack Foundation Gifts, 1976 1976.279. Alfred Stieglitz Collection, 1949 49.59.1. Purchase, Lila Acheson Wallace Gift, Arthur Hoppock Hearn Fund, Arthur Lejwa Fund in honor of Jean Arp; The Bernhill Fund, Joseph H. Hazen Foundation, Inc., Samuel I. Newhouse Foundation, Inc., Walter Bareiss, Marie Bannon McHenry, Louise Smith and Stephen C. Swid Gifts, 1980
Page 91:
Bequest of Benjamin Altman, 1913 14.40.732
Page 92:
Bequest of Miss Adelaide Milton de Groot (1876–1967), 1967 67.187.127
Page 93:
Rogers Fund, 1918 JP 1052
Page 94:
Harris Brisbane Dick Fund, 1935 35.42. Gift of Alfred Stieglitz, 1933 33.43.39
Page 95:
Hugo Kastor Fund, 1962 62.95

Page 96:
The Mr. and Mrs. Charles Kramer Collection, Gift of Mr. and Mrs. Charles Kramer, 1979 1979.620.90
Page 98:
Gift of Felix M. Warburg, 1928 28.106.23
Page 99:
Bequest of Mrs. H. O. Havemeyer, 1929, H. O. Havemeyer Collection 29.100.110
Page 100:
Rogers Fund, 1949 49.30
Page 101:
Bequest of Miss Adelaide Milton de Groot (1876–1967), 1967 67.187.87
Page 102:
Arthur Hoppock Hearn Fund, 1967 67.232. Gift of J. Pierpont Morgan, 1917 17.190.620
Page 103:
Purchase, Warner Communications Inc. Gift and matching funds from the National Endowment for the Arts, 1980 1980.1073.2 (1–2)
Page 105:
Bequest of Sam A. Lewisohn, 1951 51.112.5

INDEX OF AUTHORS AND TITLES

A Birthday, 41
Afternoon on a Hill, 77
Akan people, 23
Alighieri, Dante, 36
All the Pretty Little Horses, 22
Although I Conquer All the Earth, 33
Ambo people, 10
Anonymous, 22; 15th century, 24; China, 1st century
   B.C., 35; 39; 18th century, 40; 16th century, 49;
   17th century, 49; 50; 51; medieval, 59
Another Sarah, 19
A Nut Tree, 50
Apollinaire, Guillaume, 98, 99
A Rabbit as King of the Ghosts, 56
Ashbery, John, 64, 102
A Ternary of Littles, upon a Pipkin of Jelly Sent
   to a Lady, 39
A True Account of Talking to the Sun at Fire Island, 104
Autobiographia Literaria, 31
Autumn Cove, 61
Ballad of the Morning Streets, 83
Baraka, Amiri, 83
Bashō, 66, 79
Bavarian Gentians, 91
Bee! I'm expecting you!, 66
Berrigan, Ted, 29
Beside the road, 79
Bingo, 51
Bishop, Elizabeth, 86
Blake, William, 18, 48, 61
Bly, Robert, 82
Breton, André, 91
Breton, Nicholas, 37
Buson, 79
Butterfly, 65
Bye, Reed, 21
Byron, Lord, 72
Canticle, 95
Carroll, Lewis, 52, 53, 68
Ceravolo, Joseph, 84
Chippewa Indians, 12
Chocolate Milk, 83
Clare, John, 66
Come unto These Yellow Sands, 14
Convalescence, 84
Counting-Out Rhyme, 55
Coward, Noël, 84
Cuckoo, 81
cummings, e. e., 60, 101
Dawn, 87
de la Mare, Walter, 73
Dickinson, Emily, 19, 66, 75, 87
Dinka people, 57
Disillusionment of Ten O'clock, 90
Durfey, Thomas, 51
Egypt, Ancient, 9, 10

Elephant, *From,* 69
Eluard, Paul, 59, 68, 92
Engraved on the Collar of a Dog, Which I Gave
   to His Royal Highness, 60
Eskimo, 24
Fang people, 8
First cold rain, 79
Five Ghost Songs, 10
Fog, 94
Folksong, American, 53
For the Moment, 78
Free Union, *From,* 91
From a Childhood, 27
Frost, Robert, 76, 82
Gozzano, Guido, 88
Grasshoppers, 66
Greensleeves, 40
Ground-Squirrel Song, 57
Hardy, Thomas, 61, 73
Heart Crown and Mirror, 98
Heaven, 74
Herbert, George, 74
here's a little mouse, 60
Herrick, Robert, 16, 17, 39
Hopi Indians, 23, 63
Hopkins, Gerard Manley, 81, 101
Hops, 44
Hottentot people, 9
House Song to the East, 13
Housman, A. E., 44
How cool it feels, 79
How Doth the Little Crocodile, 68
How Marigolds Came Yellow, 16
How Violets Came Blue, 16
Hughes, Langston, 28, 46
Humpty Dumpty's Recitation, 52
Hymn to the Sun, 8
"I Am Cherry Alive," the Little Girl Sang, 54
If All the World Were Paper, 49
I Have Lived and I Have Loved, 39
I'll Sail upon the Dog-star, 51
In a Train, 82
India, Ancient, 33
Indian Serenade, 41
I Sing for the Animals, 57
Issa, 63, 79
I Stood in the Maytime Meadows, 59
I Think, 20
It's Raining, 99
It Was a Lover and His Lass, 38
I've just come up, 79
I Wandered Lonely as a Cloud, 75
I Want to Say Your Name, 45
Jabberwocky, 53
Jōsō, 79
Jubilate Agno, *From,* 62

Juke Box Love Song, 46
Keats, John, 67
Kirsten, 29
Kwakiutl Indians, 23
Lawrence, D. H., 59, 64, 65, 68, 91
Lear, Edward, 54
Leopardi, Giacomo, 72
Liberty, *From,* 92
Li Po, 34, 61, 71
Little Fish, 68
Lorca, Federico García, 28, 73, 93
Lullaby, 23
Lully, Lulla, 24
Marlowe, Christopher, 33
May rains, 79
Meditations of a Parrot, 64
Meet-on-the-Road, 50
Millay, Edna St. Vincent, 55, 77
Minnie and Winnie, 26
Miss Blues'es Child, 28
Mr. Lizard Is Crying, 93
Narcolepsy, 94
Nashe, Thomas, 15
Navaho Indians, 11, 12, 13, 57, 58
Neruda, Pablo, 69
No one spoke, 79
Oath of Friendship, 35
O Beauteous One, 10
O'Hara, Frank, 31, 47, 55, 103, 104
Oh, When I Was in Love with You, 44
One person, 79
On the Grasshopper and Cricket, 67
On the temple bell, 79
Owen, Maureen, 94
Padgett, Ron, 67, 83
Pasternak, Boris, 44
Peacock, 64
Phillida and Coridon, 37
Pied Beauty, 101
Pig, 68
Ploughing on Sunday, 100
Poem (Williams), 62
Poem (O'Hara), 103
Poem for Shane on Her Brother's Birthday, 30
Poems to the Sun, 9
Pope, Alexander, 60
Porter, Anne, 19
Pound, Ezra (after Li Po), 34
Puva, puva, puva, 23
Reverdy, Pierre, 78
Rilke, Rainer Maria, 27, 59, 89
Rimbaud, Arthur, 76, 87, 98
Roethke, Theodore, 77
Rose, Oh Pure Contradiction, 89
Rossetti, Christina, 41

Ryōta, 65, 79
Sandburg, Carl, 94
Sanders, Donald T., 30
Sanpū, 79
Schuyler, James, 20, 46, 81
Schwartz, Delmore, 54
Senghor, Léopold Sédar, 45
Sensation, 76
Shakespeare, William, 14, 15, 38, 66
Shapiro, David, 95
Shelley, Percy Bysshe, 41, 70, 72
Silly Song, 28
Silver, 73
Skelton, John, 25
Sleeping on the Ceiling, 86
Smart, Christopher, 62
Snyder, Gary, 82
Some Good Things to Be Said for the Iron Age, 82
Song (O'Hara), 47
Song (Schuyler), 81
Song Form, 83
Song for the Sun That Disappeared behind the
     Rainclouds, 9
Song of Myself, *From,* 80
Song of Parents Who Want to Wake up
     Their Son, 23
Song of the Flood, 12
Sonnet, 35
Soupault, Philippe, 102
So We'll Go No More A-Roving, 72
Spider, 66
Sporting Goods, 102
Spring (Blake), 18
Spring (Bye), 21
Spring Night in Lo-yang—Hearing a Flute, 71
Spring, the Sweet Spring, 15
Stein, Gertrude, 97
Stevens, Wallace, 56, 90, 100
Still Night Thoughts, 71
Stopping by Woods on a Snowy Evening, 76
Sunday, 46
Tender Buttons, *From,* 97
Tennyson, Alfred, Lord, 26, 43
Teton Sioux Indians, 57
The Approach of the Storm, 12
The Argument of His Book, 16
The Big Rock Candy Mountains, 53
The Cat and the Moon, 63
The Cottager to Her Infant, 26
The Elephant, 69
The Fallow Deer at the Lonely House, 61
The Great Figure, 90
The Koocoo, 49
The Letter, 43
The Locust Tree in Flower, 18

The Magnificent Bull, 57
The Moon Rises, 73
The Most Beautiful, 88
The Owl, 63
The Owl and the Pussy-cat, 54
The Passionate Shepherd to His Love, 33
The Pasture, 82
There Are No People Song, 11
The Red Wheelbarrow, 82
The River-Merchant's Wife: A Letter, 34
The Song of Kuk-ook, the Bad Boy, 24
The Song of Wandering Aengus, 89
The Thinnest Shadow, 102
The Tyger, 61
The Unicorn, *From,* 59
The Waking, 77
The War God's Horse Song, 58
The White Horse, 59
The Wind Is Blowing West, 84
The Wind Took up the Northern Things, 75
The World's Wanderers, 70
They look/Like newlyweds, 65
They Say You're Staying in a Mountain Temple, 71
Thinking of East Mountain, 71
Three Animals, 67
To an Isle in the Water, 42
To a Poor Old Woman, 81
To a Skylark, *From,* 75
To Daffodils, 17
Today, 55
To Mistress Isabel Pennell, 25
To Ride, 59
To the Moon (Leopardi), 72
To the Moon (Shelley), 72
Tu Fu, 71
Under the Greenwood Tree, 15
up into the silence the green, 101
Upon Julia's Clothes, 38
Viewing the Waterfall at Mount Lu, 71
Vowels, 98
Waiting Both, 73
We Like March, 19
Well, let's go, 79
When the Green Woods Laugh, 48
Where the Bee Sucks, 66
Whitman, Walt, 80
Who Is the East?, 87
Wild Goose, Wild Goose, 63
Williams, William Carlos, 18, 62, 81, 90
Wordsworth, Dorothy, 26
Wordsworth, William, 75
Yeats, William Butler, 42, 63, 89
Yoruba people, 69

A cool red rose and a pink cut pink, 97
A light white, a disgrace, 97
A little monkey goes like a donkey, 97
A little saint best fits a little shrine, 39
All the cattle are resting in the fields, 9
Although I conquer all the earth, 33
Among/of/green, 18
Among the rain, 90
A ringing tire iron, 82
Art thou pale for weariness, 72
A star looks down at me, 73
As the cat, 62
At Autumn Cove, so many white monkeys, 61
Bee! I'm expecting you, 66
Beneath the willow, wound round with ivy, 44
Beside the road, 79
Black A, white E, red I, green U, blue O—vowels, 98
Bluebird &/honeymoon over, 21
Brave as a postage stamp, 102
But most beautiful of all is the Un-found Island, 88
Butterfly, the wind blows sea-ward, 65
By Saint Mary, my lady, 25
Colored hats are necessary, 97
Coloring high means that the strange reason, 97
Come live with me and be my love, 33
Come unto these yellow sands, 14
Did you see me walking by the Buick Repairs, 47
Don't sleep! for your paddle fell into the water,
     and your spear, 23
During the Early Winter, 30
Elephant beaten with candy, 97
Elephant, who brings death, 69
Enthusiastically hurting a clouded yellow bud, 97
Fair daffodils we weep to see, 17
Far in the east, far below, there a house
     was made, 13
First cold rain, 79
For I will consider my Cat Jeoffrey, 62
From the half/Of the sky, 12
Glory be to God for dappled things, 101
Grasshoppers go in many a thrumming spring, 66
Greensleeves was all my joy, 40
Gross innocent, 69
Guido, I wish that you and Lapo and I, 36
He is sherrier, 102
here's a little mouse) and, 60
How cool it feels, 79
How doth the little crocodile, 68
Hushaby,/Don't you cry, 22
"I am cherry alive," the little girl sang, 54
I am his Highness' dog at Kew, 60
I am the Turquoise Woman's son, 58
I am trying to decide to go swimming, 84
I arise from dreams of thee, 41
I could take the Harlem night, 46

I embraced the summer dawn, 87
If all the world were paper, 49
If the blues would let me, 28
I had a little nut tree, 50
I have lived and I have loved, 39
I'll sail upon the Dog-star, 51
I'm about to go shopping, 81
I'm going out to clean the pasture spring, 82
In April, the koocoo can sing her song by rote, 49
In the merry month of May, 37
In what house, the jade flute that sends these
   dark notes drifting, 71
In winter, when the fields are white, 52
I remember, gracious, graceful moon, 72
I sing of brooks, of blossoms, birds, and bowers, 16
I stood in the Maytime meadows, 59
I strolled across, 77
It is so peaceful on the ceiling, 86
It's been so long since I headed for
   East Mountain, 71
It's raining women's voices, 99
It was a lover, and his lass, 38
I've just come up, 79
I wandered lonely as a cloud, 75
I want to say your name, Naëtt!, 45
I was on a white coast once, 95
I went out to the hazel wood, 89
I will be the gladdest thing, 77
I will write you a letter, 20
Jealous girls these sometimes were, 16
Life is simple and gay, 78
Love on a day (wise poets tell), 16
Lully, lulla, thou little tiny child, 24
Mama,/I wish I were silver, 28
May rains, 79
Minnie and Winnie, 26
Moonlight in front of my bed, 71
Morning uptown, quiet on the street, 83
Mr. lizard is crying, 93
Munching a plum on/the street, 81
My bull is white like the silver fish in the river, 57
My heart is like a singing bird, 41
My heart like an upside down flame, 98
My wife whose hair is a brush fire, 91
No one spoke, 79
Not every man has gentians in his house, 91
"Now, pray, where are you going, child?"
   said Meet on-the-Road, 50
O beauteous one, O cow, O great one, 10
Oh God! It's great, 83
Oh! kangaroos, sequins, chocolate sodas, 55
Oh the rocks and the thimble, 64
Oh this is the animal that never was, 59
Oh, when I was in love with you, 44
On blue summer evenings I'll go
   down the pathways, 76

One evening as the sun went down, 53
One person, 79
One without looks in tonight, 61
On my school notebooks, 92
On the temple bell, 79
O solo mio, hot diggety, nix "I wather think
   I can," 103
Out of the earth, 57
O who will show me those delights on high, 74
Puva, puva, puva, 23
Repeat that, repeat, 81
Rose, oh pure contradiction, joy, 89
Shang ya!/I want to be your friend, 35
Shy one, shy one, 42
Silver bark of beech, and sallow, 55
Slowly, silently, now the moon, 73
Someone would like to have you for her child, 23
So much depends, 81
Sound the flute, 18
So, we'll go no more a-roving, 72
Spring, the sweet spring, is the year's
   pleasant king, 15
Sunlight streaming on Incense Stone kindles
   violet smoke, 71
Tell me, thou Star, whose wings of light, 70
The butterfly/flies up like pow, 67
The cat went here and there, 63
The darkening was like riches in the room, 27
The days are cold, the nights are long, 26
The difficulty to think at the end of day, 56
The dove stays in the garden, 10
The fearful night sinks, 8
The fire darkens, the wood turns black, 9
The first man—you are his child, he is
   your child, 12
The fog comes, 94
The houses are haunted, 90
The magic of the day is the morning, 83
The miller's mill-dog lay at the mill-door, 51
The mint bed is in/bloom, 46
The Owl and the Pussy-cat went to sea, 54
The owl hooted and told of the morning star, 63
The poetry of earth is never dead, 67
The pure contralto sings in the organloft, 80
There has been a light snow, 83
The squirrel in his shirt, 57
The street is soon there, 59
The sun like a sleepy giant, 94
The Sun woke me this morning loud, 104
The tiny fish enjoy themselves, 68
The white cock's tail, 100
The Wind took up the Northern Things, 75
They look/Like newlyweds, 65
The youth walks up to the white horse, to put
   its halter on, 59
They say you're staying in a mountain temple, 71

Think how a peacock in a forest of high trees, 64
This is the song of Kuk-ook, the bad boy, 24
To have been a little ill, 84
'Twas brillig, and the slithy toves, 53
Tyger! Tyger! burning bright, 61
Under the greenwood tree, 15
up into the silence the green, 101
Up with me! up with me into the clouds, 75
We like March—his shoes are Purple, 19
Well, let's go, 79
Whenas in silks my Julia goes, 38
When I was a child, 31
When the green woods laugh with the voice of joy, 48
When the moon comes up, 73
When winter was half over, 19
Where is another sweet as my sweet, 43
Where the bee sucks, there suck I, 66
While my hair was still cut straight across my
   forehead, 34
Who is the East, 87
Whose woods these are I think I know, 76
Wild goose, wild goose, 63
With sun on his back and sun on his belly, 68
With what voice, 66
you're so funny! I'd give you, 29
You say there were no people, 11